The Fix

Since 1996, Bloomberg Press has published books for financial professionals, as well as books of general interest in investing, economics, current affairs, and policy affecting investors and business people. Titles are written by well-known practitioners, Bloomberg News® reporters and columnists, and other leading authorities and journalists. Bloomberg Press books have been translated into more than 20 languages.

For a list of available titles, please visit our website at www.wiley.com/go/bloombergpress.

The Fix

How Bankers Lied, Cheated and Colluded to Rig the World's Most Important Number

Liam Vaughan
and Gavin Finch

WILEY | **Bloomberg** PRESS

This edition first published 2017
© 2017 Liam Vaughan and Gavin Finch

Registered office

John Wiley & Sons Ltd, The Atrium, Southern Gate, Chichester, West Sussex, PO19 8SQ, United Kingdom

For details of our global editorial offices, for customer services and for information about how to apply for permission to reuse the copyright material in this book please visit our website at www.wiley.com.

Wiley publishes in a variety of print and electronic formats and by print-on-demand. Some material included with standard print versions of this book may not be included in e-books or in print-on-demand. If this book refers to media such as a CD or DVD that is not included in the version you purchased, you may download this material at http://booksupport.wiley.com. For more information about Wiley products, visit www.wiley.com.

Designations used by companies to distinguish their products are often claimed as trademarks. All brand names and product names used in this book are trade names, service marks, trademarks or registered trademarks of their respective owners. The publisher is not associated with any product or vendor mentioned in this book.

A catalogue record for this book is available from the Library of Congress.

A catalogue record for this book is available from the British Library.

ISBN 978-1-118-99572-3 (hardback)   ISBN 978-1-118-99573-0 (ePub)
ISBN 978-1-118-99574-7 (ePDF)   ISBN 978-1-118-99575-4 (O-book)

Cover design: Wiley
Cover image: City image © Petr Student/Shutterstock; Puppet image © Rudek/Shutterstock

10 9 8 7 6 5 4 3 2

Set in 11.5/14pt BemboStd by Aptara Inc., New Delhi, India
Printed in the United States of America by LSC Communications, Harrisonburg, VA, U.S.A.

To Robert, a class act

Contents

Introduction

There were four of us at a table by the bar, eyeing each other with suspicion: two reporters, a highly paid derivatives trader in his early thirties, and a lawyer who had cautiously brokered the meeting. We'd just written a story about how the trader and a handful of his colleagues had been sacked, and he was incensed. His reputation was ruined, and he was aggravated by what he saw as the fundamental ignorance of the press. Did we even understand what Libor was? Did we understand what Libor had become?

On that chilly afternoon in February 2012, at a near-empty hotel bar in central London, the word "Libor" had not yet entered the public vernacular. In the world of finance, it was common. Libor was the name of a benchmark interest rate, one that was both mundane—it was just a measure of how much it cost banks to borrow from each other—and extraordinary. Libor was in *everything*, from mortgages in Alabama to business loans in Liverpool to the hundreds of billions of dollars in bailout money given to banks during the financial crisis. It was sometimes called the "world's most important number", and the trader sitting across from us was accused of trying to manipulate it.[1] From his body language it was clear he didn't want to be here, but he was desperate. So were we. We didn't even know his name.[2]

"Why do you need to know that?" he snapped when we asked. He had heavy bags under his dark, narrow eyes. All we needed to appreciate, the trader insisted, was that Libor wasn't what we thought it was. "There are no rules," he said, avoiding eye contact. "There never have been. This is all a fucking joke." When we pressed him for specifics, he clammed up. After the second round of drinks arrived, we tried a different approach. What was it we didn't understand?

The trader shook his head impatiently. Discussing Libor with colleagues and counterparts was as much a part of life on the trading floor as debauched nights out and crude language, he said. It had been going on forever and was widely condoned by management. But it had gotten more complicated than that, he continued. Libor had broken down. It was supposed to be a measure of how much lenders paid each other to borrow cash, but since the crisis, banks no longer lent to each other at all. Libor had become a fictional construct, dreamed up each day in the minds of a group of bankers with a vested interest in where it was set. The world's most important number was a fraud.

After an hour and a half, the trader relented and gave us his name. We asked if we could meet again and struck a deal: If we promised never to mention our meetings in our articles, he said he would guide us through the secretive, close-knit world of derivatives trading—a rarefied ecosystem where mathematically gifted young men bet billions of dollars of their employers' money on movements in complex securities few people understand, then come together in restaurants and clubs in the evenings to enjoy the spoils.

The party was ending fast. A few days earlier, the first official document alleging Libor manipulation at a group of major banks had leaked. The affidavit filed by antitrust authorities in a court in Canada was light on details and, beyond a few brief news items, attracted little interest from the mainstream media. Still, we were intrigued. One of the more shocking aspects of the case was that the traders involved worked for the very banks whose recklessness had helped bring the global financial system to its knees in 2008. We had listened to kowtowing executives from bailed-out behemoths like UBS, Royal Bank of Scotland and Citigroup tell the public how they had reformed. If the Libor allegations were true, rather than learning their lesson, the banks were behaving worse than ever.

Six traders and brokers were named in the Canadian document, but the individual who was pulling the strings—the kingpin at the center of the conspiracy—was referred to only as Trader A. This was tantalizing. How had he done it? How had one man managed to shift one of the central pillars of the financial system in the years when the banking authorities were supposedly at their most vigilant? And what kind of individual would have the chutzpah to even try?

At the bar in London, before we parted ways, we asked the trader one final question: "Who is Trader A?"

"Pretty sure that's Tom Hayes," he said. "He's just some weird, quiet kid who completely owned the market before he blew up."

■ ■ ■

By the summer of 2012, Libor was front-page news. In June, Barclays became the first bank to reach a settlement with authorities around the world, admitting to rigging the rate and agreeing to pay a then-record £290 million ($355 million) in fines. The British lender avoided criminal charges thanks to its extensive cooperation with the investigation, but the fallout was devastating. The scandal coincided with the eurozone debt crisis and a renewed period of seething disdain for the banking sector. News bulletins cut from riots in Athens and Occupy Wall Street protests in New York to transcripts of traders calling each other "big boy" and agreeing to defraud the public for a "bottle of Bollinger". Within a week, Barclays's charismatic chief executive officer, Bob Diamond, had been forced to resign, and the reputation of the Bank of England, which was accused of being directly involved in the U.K. lender's behavior, was in shreds.

Barclays bore the worst of the public opprobrium, but it wasn't alone. Swiss lender UBS settled with the authorities in December, followed quickly by taxpayer-owned RBS, Dutch bank Rabobank and interdealer brokers ICAP and RP Martin. To date, about a dozen firms and more than 100 individuals have been implicated from all over the world. In an era defined by the breakdown in trust between banks and the rest of society, Libor has confirmed people's worst suspicions about the financial system: That behind closed doors, shrouded in complexity and protected by weak and complicit regulators, armies of bankers are gleefully spending their days screwing us over.

The reality is both more complex and more shocking than that. The picture that emerges over thousands of pages of public and leaked documents and hundreds of interviews we conducted—with the traders and brokers involved in the scandal, the regulators and central bankers who failed to curb them, and the small, tenacious band of U.S. investigators who ultimately brought them to account—is of a system in which manipulation was not just possible but inevitable. Everyone must take their share of responsibility: the bank executives who fostered a culture where making money trumped all else; the authorities too weak or unwilling to ask awkward questions; and the governments, giddy on tax receipts, who ushered in a style of laissez-faire regulation whose disastrous effects are still being felt today.

At its heart, though, this is a story about a group of traders and brokers who found a flaw in the machine and exploited it for all it was worth. Despite their actions, the men who shared their stories with us are not one-dimensional hucksters unburdened by a conscience. For the most part, they are smart, likeable men—and they are all men—who love their children and cry at sad movies and who somewhere along the way convinced themselves that responsibility for their behavior lay with the system rather than themselves.

As we were putting this book together, the doping allegations against Tour de France legend Lance Armstrong were emerging. The parallels were striking. Within the closed ranks of both banking and cycling, the bounds of what constituted acceptable behavior had diverged over time from the rest of society, cleaved by a heady mix of testosterone, competition, groupthink, lax oversight and skewed incentives. Both worlds also had their antiheroes—individuals who, through sheer will and force of personality, went further than anyone else, dragging behind them an entourage of enablers and co-conspirators.

In the case of Libor, the antihero is Tom Hayes: a brilliant, obsessive, reckless, irascible math prodigy who transformed rate-rigging from a blunt instrument into a thing of intricate, terrible beauty. A socially awkward misfit in his early years, he found his calling the moment he walked onto a trading floor, where the idiosyncrasies that had dogged him his whole life became assets. They made him a fortune before they sealed his downfall. This is his journey. This is the story of Trader A.

Chapter 1

The End of the World

At the Tokyo headquarters of a Swiss bank, in the middle of a deserted trading floor, Tom Hayes sat rapt before a bank of eight computer screens. Collar askew, pale features pinched, blond hair mussed from a habit of pulling at it when he was deep in thought, the British trader was even more disheveled than usual. It was Sept. 15, 2008, and it looked, in Hayes's mind, like the end of the world.

Hayes had been awakened at dawn in his apartment by a call from his boss, telling him to get into the office immediately. In New York, Lehman Brothers was hurtling toward bankruptcy. At his desk, Hayes watched the world process the news and panic. Each market as it opened became a sea of flashing red as investors frantically dumped their holdings. In moments like this, Hayes entered an almost unconscious state, rapidly processing the tide of information before him and calculating the best escape route.

Hayes was a phenom at UBS, one of the best the bank had at trading derivatives. So far, the mounting financial crisis had actually been good for him. The chaos had let him buy cheaply from those desperate to get out and sell high to the unlucky few who still needed to trade. While most dealers closed up shop in fear, Hayes, with a seemingly limitless appetite for risk, stayed in. He was 28, and he was up more than $70 million for the year.

Now that was under threat. Not only did Hayes have to extract himself from every deal he'd done with Lehman, but he'd also made a series of enormous bets that in the coming days interest rates would remain stable. The collapse of the fourth-largest investment bank in the U.S. would surely cause those rates, which were really just barometers of risk, to spike. As Hayes examined his tradebook, one rate mattered more than any other: the London interbank offered rate, or Libor, a benchmark that influences $350 trillion of securities and loans around the world. For traders like Hayes, this number was the Holy Grail. And two years earlier, he had discovered a way to rig it.

Libor was set by a self-selected, self-policing committee of the world's largest banks. The rate measured how much it cost them to borrow from each other. Every morning, each bank submitted an estimate, an average was taken and a number was published at midday. The process was repeated in different currencies, and for various amounts of time, ranging from overnight to a year. During his time as a junior trader in London, Hayes had gotten to know several of the 16 individuals responsible for making their bank's daily submission for the Japanese yen. His flash of insight was realizing that these men mostly relied on interdealer brokers, the fast-talking middlemen involved in every trade, for guidance on what to submit each day.

Hayes saw what no one else did because he was different. His intimacy with numbers, his cold embrace of risk and his manias were more than professional tics; they were signs that he'd been wired differently since birth. Hayes would not be diagnosed with Asperger's syndrome until 2015, when he was 35, but his co-workers, many of them savvy operators from fancy schools, often reminded Hayes that he wasn't like them. They called him "Rain Man".[1] Most traders looked down on brokers as second-class citizens, too. Hayes recognized their worth. He'd been paying some of them to lie ever since.

By the time the market opened in London, Lehman's demise was official. Hayes instant-messaged one of his trusted brokers in the U.K. capital to tell him what direction he wanted Libor to move. Typically, he skipped any pleasantries. "Cash mate, really need it lower," Hayes typed. "What's the score?" The broker sent his assurances and, over the next few hours, followed a well-worn playbook. Whenever one of the Libor-setting banks called and asked his opinion on what the benchmark would do, the broker said—incredibly, given the calamitous news—that the rate was likely to fall. Libor may have featured in hundreds of trillions of dollars of loans and derivatives, but this was how it was set: conversations among men who were, depending on the day, indifferent, optimistic or frightened. When Hayes checked the official figures later that night, he saw to his inexpressible relief that yen Libor had fallen.

Hayes was not out of danger yet. Over the next three days, he barely left the office, surviving on three hours of sleep a night. As the market convulsed, his profit and loss jumped around from minus $20 million to plus $8 million in just hours, but Hayes had another ace up his sleeve. ICAP, the world's biggest interdealer broker, sent out a "Libor prediction" e-mail each morning at around 7 a.m. to the individuals at the banks responsible for submitting Libor. Hayes messaged an insider at the firm and instructed him to skew the predictions lower. Amid the bedlam, Libor was the one thing Hayes believed he had some control over. He cranked his network to the max, offering his brokers extra payments for their cooperation and calling in favors at banks around the world. By Thursday, Sept. 18, Hayes was exhausted. This was the moment he'd been working toward all week. If Libor jumped today, his puppeteering would have been for naught. Libor moves in increments called basis points, equal to one one-hundredth of a percentage point, and every tick was worth roughly $750,000 to his bottom line.

For the umpteenth time since Lehman faltered, Hayes reached out to his brokers in London. "I need you to keep it as low as possible, all right?" he told one of them in a message. "I'll pay you, you know, $50,000, $100,000, whatever. Whatever you want, all right?"

"All right," the broker repeated.

"I'm a man of my word," Hayes said.

"I know you are. No, that's done, right, leave it to me," the broker said.

Hayes was still in the office when that day's Libors were published at noon in London, 8 p.m. in Tokyo. The yen rate had fallen 1 basis point, while comparable money market rates in other currencies continued to soar. Hayes's crisis had been averted. Using his network, he had personally sought to tilt part of the planet's financial infrastructure. He pulled off his headset and headed home to bed. He'd only recently upgraded from the superhero duvet he'd slept under since he was eight years old.

Chapter 2

Tommy Chocolate

Thomas Alexander William Hayes had always been an outsider. Born in 1979 and raised in the urban sprawl of Hammersmith, West London, Hayes was bright but found it hard to connect with other kids. His parents divorced when he was in primary school. When his mother Sandra remarried, she took Hayes and his younger brother Robin to live with her new husband, a management consultant, and his two children in the leafy, affluent commuter town of Winchester, bordering a stretch of bucolic countryside in the south of England. The couple fostered a child and later had a daughter of their own. They bought a big house on a pretty street lined with them. It was always full.

Hayes's mother was a naturally timid woman, and when Hayes misbehaved or became angry, she did everything she could to placate him. From an early age few people said no to him. In his teenage years, Hayes saw less of his father Nick, a left-wing journalist and documentary filmmaker who relocated to Manchester in the north of the country with his girlfriend, a crossword writer for *The Guardian* newspaper. Hayes attended Westgate, a well-regarded state secondary school a 10-minute walk from his new home, and then Peter Symonds, a sixth-form college that was even closer. His college math teacher, Tania Zeigler, remembers him as a "kind, thoughtful and normal" student.[1] Hayes achieved good grades but had a small circle of friends. Awkward and quiet, with lank, scraggly hair and acne, he rarely socialized and wouldn't learn to drive until he was in his thirties. When he did venture to the pub, he usually had one eye on the slot machines, waiting to pounce after someone else had emptied his pockets. Surrounded by the children of well-to-do professionals, he held onto his inner-city London accent, traveling back on weekends to watch his beloved football team, the perennial underdogs Queens Park Rangers.

Hayes was a decent footballer, but from a young age favored solitary pastimes that fostered his natural ability for mathematics: computer games, puzzles and an ardent devotion to QPR, which offered a nerd's paradise of statistics, history and results to pore over. Fixations—along with social problems, elevated stress levels and a propensity for numbers over words—are a symptom of Asperger's, but in the years before works like *The Imitation Game* and *The Curious Incident of the Dog in the Night-Time* made the condition better understood, Hayes just struck people as withdrawn.

Hayes remained a peripheral figure at the University of Nottingham, where he studied math and engineering. While his fellow students took their summer holidays, he worked 90-hour weeks cleaning pots and pulling pints behind the bar of a local pub for £2.70 an hour. He had no desire to go abroad when he could be earning money. Even when carrying out menial tasks, he prided himself on his dedication. "It didn't matter whether I was cleaning a deep fat fryer or deboning a chicken, those jobs got left to me because they knew there would be no chicken left on the bone and there would be no fat in the fryer," Hayes would later explain. "That's just the way I am."[2]

Toward the end of his course he secured a 10-week internship at UBS in London, working on the collateral-management desk, a mundane but complex station where it was difficult to stand out. But Hayes did, and the Swiss bank offered him a full-time role when he finished his studies. Hayes turned it down in order to find a trading position. That's where the real excitement was.

After graduating in 2001, Hayes got his wish, joining the rapidly expanding RBS as a trainee on the interest-rate derivatives desk. For 20 minutes a day, as a reward for making the tea and collecting dry cleaning, he was allowed to ask the traders anything he wanted. It was an epiphany. Unlike the messy interactions and hidden agendas that characterized day-to-day life, the formula for success in finance was clear: Make money and everything else will follow. It became Hayes's guiding principle, and he began to read voraciously about markets, options-pricing models, interest rate curves, and other financial arcana.

Within a year Hayes was given a small trading book to look after while its main trader in Asia was away from the office. His risk limits were tiny, but it gave Hayes real-time exposure to the financial instruments, such as swaps, that he would go on to master. His timing was perfect. Swaps, in which parties agree to exchange a floating rate of interest for a fixed one, were originally used to protect companies from fluctuations in interest rates. By the time Hayes arrived they were mostly bought and sold between professional traders at banks and hedge funds, another high-stakes security to wager the future on. In 1998, about $36 trillion of the instruments changed hands. Within seven years that had exploded to $169 trillion. By the end of the decade it was closer to $349 trillion.[3] It was a gold rush.

In the laddish, hedonistic culture of the markets, the 21-year-old Hayes was an odd fit. On the rare occasions he joined bankers and brokers on their nights out, Hayes stuck to hot chocolate. They called him "Tommy Chocolate" behind his back and blurted out *Rain Man* quotes like "Qantas never crashed" as Hayes shuffled round the trading floor. He was bad at banter, given to taking quips and digs at face value. The superhero duvet was a particular point of derision. The bedding was perfectly adequate, Hayes thought; he didn't see the point in buying another one.

There were also signs of his soon-to-be notorious temper. According to one story that made its way round the City of London, Hayes began seeing a woman from his office and one night arranged to make her dinner. Hayes cooked, while his date had a bath. When he'd finished, he called for her to join him. After asking for a third time, Hayes became so irritated he barged into the bathroom and poured a dish of shepherd's pie into the bath with her. The episode quickly entered trading floor legend, and traders and brokers took to hollering "aye aye shepherd's pie" and "get in the bath!".

At work, the complex calculations and constant mental exertion involved in trading derivatives came easily, but Hayes found he had something rarer: a steely stomach for risk. While other new recruits looked to book their gains or curb short-term losses, Hayes rode volatile market movements like a seasoned rodeo rider. In those early years he hit the dirt as often as he was successful, but his talent was clear and in 2004 he was headhunted by Royal Bank of Canada, a smaller outfit where Hayes could take a position of prominence and rise more quickly.

RBC's London operation wasn't set up to trade the full gamut of derivatives products, so Hayes spent the first year or so working with a team of quantitative analysts and IT specialists to bring the bank's systems up to his standards. Hayes was a perfectionist, and, still in his early twenties, he helped the firm design a platform that could monitor minute shifts in profit and loss and risk exposure in real time—a set-up more advanced than at many of the biggest players in the market. It was a process Hayes would go on to repeat each time he started at a new firm.

Finally, Hayes was satisfied, and he leapt into the market with his own trading book. Traders at the largest firms recall suddenly seeing minnow RBC taking the other side of big-ticket deals. Hayes may have been baffled by the simple rituals of office camaraderie, but when he looked at the convoluted world of yen derivatives he saw clarity. "The success of getting it right, the success of finding market inefficiencies, the success of identifying opportunities and then when you get it right—it's like solving that equation," Hayes would later explain in his nasal, pedantic delivery. "It's make money, lose money, and it's just so pure."[4]

In poker, there are two types of player: tight folk who wait for the best cards, then bet big and hope to get paid; and hawks who can't resist getting involved in every hand, needling opponents and scaring the nervous ones into folding. Hayes was firmly in the latter camp. His M.O. was to trade constantly, picking up snippets of information, racking up commissions as a market maker and building a persona as a high-volume, high-stakes risk-taker.

Hayes's success on the trading floor brought a newfound confidence to the naturally reticent young man. Trading is primarily a solitary pursuit, one individual's battle against the world, armed only with his guile, a bank of screens and a phone. Still, among the derivative traders and quants Hayes found kindred spirits, people for whom systems and patterns were second nature and who shared his passion for financial markets and economics. He was quick to dismiss those he considered lacking in talent. Salespeople—the polished, mostly privately educated, multilingual young men and women drafted in droves by prestigious investment banks to be their public face—were given particularly short shrift.

As a state-school-educated Londoner with a cockney twang and a love of football, Hayes felt he had more in common with the mostly working-class interdealer brokers who matched up buyers and sellers. Naturally suspicious of other people's intentions, Hayes took months before he warmed to a broker. Once he did, he called him incessantly, prodding him for information about rivals at other firms and scolding him if he felt he was getting quoted poor prices. If he pushed too far, slamming down the phone or dishing out profanities, he would call back to apologize and throw some extra business the broker's way. Hayes was loyal to those he considered to be on his side and merciless with anyone he didn't. Everything was black and white. The contacts he made early in his career at the banks and interdealer brokers in London would play a pivotal role later when his gaze fixed firmly on Libor.

For all the ribbing Hayes took on the trading floor, he had found a place where he belonged. He rose early, worked at least 12 hours a day and rarely stayed awake past 10 p.m. He often got up to check his trading positions during the night. And ultimately, Hayes went along with the jokes because the obsessive traits that had marginalized him socially turned into assets the moment he logged on to his terminal.

In the spring of 2006, a headhunter put Hayes in touch with an Australian banker named Anthony Robson who was recruiting for his sales desk at UBS. The pair met in a quiet corner of a branch of Corney & Barrow, a chain of basement haunts popular with City of London bankers where deals are forged over pints of ale and pie and mash. Within five minutes it was obvious to Robson that Hayes, with his scruffy demeanor and idiosyncrasies, wasn't suited to a client-facing role. But there was something undeniably intriguing about the blond-haired kid who barely broke for breath. For an hour and a half they talked about trading methodologies, interest-rate curves and derivatives pricing models. Hayes spoke with a zeal and depth of knowledge that left Robson astounded. When the meeting was over, Robson was convinced he'd met one of the most gifted individuals he'd ever interviewed. That night he put Hayes in contact with one of his counterparts in Tokyo.

In March 2006, the Japanese central bank had announced plans to curb overheating in the economy by raising interest rates for the first time in more than a decade. The move brought volatility to money markets that had been dormant, spurring a wave of buying and selling in cash, forwards and short-term interest-rate derivatives. Keen to capitalize, UBS was putting together a small team of front-end traders, who dealt in instruments that matured within two or three years. Hayes would be the perfect addition. At the time, yen was still considered something of a backwater within the banks, a steppingstone on the way to the big leagues of trading dollars or euros. The market was full of inexperienced traders not savvy enough to know when they were being fleeced. Hayes was nervous about moving to the other side of the world but sensed it was too good an opportunity to pass up.

RBS, RBC, UBS—the name on the door mattered little to Hayes, as long as he had the bank's balance sheet to wager. That summer he packed up his belongings, said goodbye to his family and boarded a flight to Tokyo. It was a major promotion that officially retired his image as a cocoa-sipping, blankie-clutching eccentric and recognized him for what he'd become: an aggressive and formidable trader. Headquartered in Zurich, UBS was a powerhouse, combining a vast balance sheet with a hard-charging Wall Street ethos and the freedom afforded by a hands-off Swiss regulator. The culture was aggressive and, as would later be proved, fatally predisposed to corruption.[5] Traders were king, and as long as they were making money, few questions were asked.

Hayes found a small apartment a short subway ride to UBS's Tokyo headquarters. His girlfriend, a young British saleswoman he'd met at RBS named Sarah Ainsworth, moved to Tokyo with Calyon Securities around the same time. The relationship petered out. The couple never saw each other. One or two old contacts from London and some particularly persistent brokers dragged Hayes out for a pint now and then amid the neon lights of Tokyo, where a wealthy young expat could have some serious fun, but Hayes was irritatingly distracted company. He had developed a more rarefied addiction.

Interest-rate swaps, forward rate agreements, basis swaps, overnight indexed swaps—the menu of complex financial instruments Hayes bought and sold came in a thousand varieties, but they shared one thing in common: Their value rose and fell with reference to benchmark interest rates, and, in particular, to Libor. Where Libor would land the next day was the great unknowable. Yet it was the difference between success and failure, profit or loss, glory or ignominy. Trading, like any other form of gambling, involves attempting to build a sense of the future based on incomplete and evolving information: rumor, historic market behavior, macroeconomic events, business flows elsewhere inside the bank. The better information a trader has, the greater his edge and the more money he can make. It became Hayes's mission to control the chaos around him, to eradicate the shades of gray. "I used to dream about Libor," Hayes said years later. "They were my bread and butter, you know. They were the instrument that underlined everything that I traded ... I was obsessed."[6]

Chapter 3

Beware of Greeks
Bearing Gifts

In 1969, Neil Armstrong walked on the moon, Richard Nixon became president of the United States and 400,000 hippies descended on a sleepy farm near Woodstock. On the other side of the Atlantic, on a winter's day in London, a mustachioed Greek banker named Minos Zombanakis was taking his own small step into the history books. He had hit upon a novel way to loan large amounts of money to companies and countries that wanted to borrow dollars but would rather avoid the rigors of U.S. financial regulation.

As the sun set over the rooftops of London's West End, Zombanakis was standing by his desk in Manufacturers Hanover's[1] new top floor office, drinking champagne and eating caviar with Iran's central bank governor, Khodadad Farmanfarmaian. Zombanakis had just pulled off the biggest coup of his career with the signing of an $80 million loan for the cash-strapped Shah of Iran. The Iranians had brought the beluga caviar and Zombanakis the vintage champagne—the party went on into the night.

The Iranian loan was one of the first ever to charge a variable rate of interest that reflected changing market conditions and be split among a group of banks. It was just as revolutionary in the staid world of 1960s banking as the moon landing, though celebrated with less fanfare, and it marked the birth of the London interbank offered rate, or Libor.

"I felt a sense of achievement to set up the whole thing, but I didn't think we were breaking ground for a new period in the financial world," says Zombanakis, now 90 and living back in Kalyves, on the island of Crete, amid the same olive groves his family has tended for generations. "We just needed a rate for the syndicated-loan market that everyone would be happy with. When you start these things, you never know how they are going to end up, how they are going to be used."

Much like the rate he created, Zombanakis had a humble start in life. The second of seven children, he'd grown up in a house with dirt floors and no electricity or running water.[2] Zombanakis left home at 17, fleeing Nazi-occupied Crete in a smuggler's open-topped boat to make the 200-mile journey to enroll at the University of Athens. Short of money, he quit in his second year and found work distributing aid for the recently arrived British Army, having stopped a soldier in the street and asked for a job. After leaving Greece, Zombanakis made his way to Harvard, where, with characteristic charm, he managed to talk himself onto a postgraduate course despite not having the necessary qualifications. From Harvard he moved to Rome and entered the world of banking as "Manny Hanny's" representative for the Middle East.

The real action, though, was happening elsewhere. By now London was growing as a global financial hub. Russia, China and many Arab states wanted to keep their dollars out of the U.S. for political reasons, or out of fear they might be confiscated, and they chose to bank their money in the U.K. instead. The City of London was also benefiting from stringent U.S. regulations that capped how much American banks could pay for dollar deposits and cut the amount of interest they could charge on bonds sold to foreigners. Many firms set up offshore offices in swinging London, where they could ply their international trade unhindered. After 10 years in Rome, Zombanakis was bored and scented an opportunity to further his career.

The eurodollar market, as the vast pool of U.S. dollars held by banks outside the U.S. is known, was already well developed, but Zombanakis had spotted a gap—the supply of large loans to borrowers looking for an alternate source of capital to the bond markets. In 1968, he persuaded his bosses in New York to give him £5 million to set up a new branch in

London. Six-foot-three and impeccably turned out, Zombanakis made a striking impression, and before long he became known in clubby British financial circles as simply the "Greek Banker". He was one of a small band of international financiers who were opening up the world's markets to cross-border lending for the first time since the Wall Street crash of 1929.

Zombanakis first met Farmanfarmaian in Beirut in 1956, and the two had hit it off. So when the Iranians needed money, they headed straight to Manufacturers Hanover's office on Upper Brook Street in London's exclusive Mayfair district.[3]

Zombanakis knew that no single firm would loan $80 million to a developing country that didn't have enough foreign-currency reserves to cover the debt. So he set about marketing the deal to a variety of foreign and domestic banks that could each take a slice of the risk. But with U.K. interest rates at 8 percent and inflation on the rise, banks were wary of committing to lending at a fixed rate for long periods—borrowing costs could increase in the interim and leave them out of pocket.

Zombanakis and his team came up with a solution: charging borrowers an interest rate recalculated every few months and funding the loan with a series of rolling deposits. The formula was simple. The banks in the syndicate would report their funding costs just before a loan-rollover date. The weighted average, rounded to the nearest 1/8th of a percentage point plus a spread for profit, became the price of the loan for the next period. Zombanakis called it the London interbank offered rate.

Other financiers cottoned on, and by 1982 the syndicated-loan market had ballooned to about $46 billion.[4] Virtually all those loans used Libor to calculate the interest charged. Soon, the rate was adopted by bankers outside the loan market who were looking for an elegant proxy for bank borrowing costs that was simple, fair and appeared to be independent. In 1970, the financier Evan Galbraith, who would go on to be U.S. ambassador to France under President Ronald Reagan, is said to have come up with the idea of pegging the first bond to Libor—known as a floating-rate note.

As London's financial markets took off, they became increasingly complex. Within a few years, Libor had morphed from being a tool to price individual loans and bonds to being a benchmark for derivatives deals worth hundreds of billions of dollars. Chief among these new

derivatives was the interest-rate swap, which allowed companies to miti-
gate the risk of fluctuating interest rates. The swap was invented during a
period of extreme volatility in global rates in the 1970s and early 1980s.[5]
The concept is simple: Two parties agree to exchange interest payments
on a set amount for a fixed period. In its most basic and common form,
one pays a fixed rate, in the belief that interest rates will rise, while the
other pays a floating rate, betting they will fall. The floating leg of the
contract is pegged, more often than not, to Libor. It wasn't just company
treasurers who bought them. Because swaps require little capital up front,
they gave traders a much cheaper way to speculate on interest-rate moves
than government bonds. Before long, banks had built up huge residual
positions in the instruments.

As Libor became more central to the global financial system, pressure
grew to codify the setting of the rate, which was still hashed out on an ad
hoc basis by the various banks involved with individual deals. In October
1984, the British Bankers' Association, a lobbying group set up in 1919
to champion the interests of U.K. financial firms, began consulting with
the Bank of England and others on how such a benchmark might work.

Several early versions of the rate evolved into BBA Libor, set in
pounds, dollars and yen, in 1986. The BBA established a panel of banks
that would be polled each day and tweaked the original formula to strip
out the bottom and top quartile of quotes to discourage cheating. Otherwise the rate looked similar to the one first conceived by Zombanakis.
In the quarter-century between then and Hayes's time at UBS, the suite
of currencies was expanded to 10 and the process became electronic, but
not much else changed.

The same could not be said of the U.K. banking industry, which was
transformed by Prime Minister Margaret Thatcher's "Big Bang" financial deregulation program of 1986. Overnight, Thatcher cleared the way
for retail banks to set up integrated investment banks that could make
markets, advise clients, sell them securities and place their own side bets,
all under one roof. She also removed obstacles to foreign banks taking
over U.K. firms, leading to an influx of big U.S. and international lenders
that brought with them a more aggressive, cutthroat ethos. The advent
of light-touch regulation, with markets more or less left to police themselves, made London a highly attractive place to do business. The market
for derivatives, bonds and syndicated loans exploded.

By the 1990s, Libor was baked into the system as the benchmark for everything from mortgages and student loans to swaps. However, it was its adoption by the Chicago Mercantile Exchange (CME) as the reference rate for eurodollar futures contracts that cemented its position at the heart of the financial markets.

Eurodollar futures are standardized, exchange-traded derivatives that let traders bet on the direction of short-term interest rates. For years, the value of the contracts was determined by a benchmark calculated by the CME, but in January 1997 the exchange ditched its own rate in favor of the now ubiquitous Libor.[6] The eurodollar futures market had been around since 1981, and the CME's highly liquid contract was particularly popular among traders looking to hedge their exposure to over-the-counter swaps. As swaps, and much else besides, referenced Libor, the CME believed its product would be more appealing if it used the same rate. Average daily trading volume at the time of the switch in 1996 was about 400,000 contracts. That rose to 2.8 million by March 2014.[7]

While the majority of market participants didn't raise an eyebrow over the CME's transition to Libor, at least two bank insiders did warn regulators it was a dangerous move.[8] One was Marcy Engel, a lawyer at Salomon Brothers, who wrote to the U.S. derivatives regulator, the Commodity Futures Trading Commission (CFTC), in late 1996 warning it would encourage cheating among traders. "A bank might be tempted to adjust its bids and offers very near the survey time in such a way as to benefit its own positions," Engel wrote. The other Cassandra was Richard Robb, a 36-year-old interest-rate trader at DKB Financial Products in New York, who suggested in a letter to the CFTC that firms might be tempted to lowball their submissions during periods of stress to mask any funding difficulties. "Even back then, it seemed to me that Libor was vulnerable to mischief," says Robb, now CEO of money manager Christofferson, Robb & Co. and a professor at Columbia University. "It was ripe to explode. It was constructed in a shabby way that was fine for its original purpose, but when it became so dominant it should have been strengthened and put on firmer foundations."

The CFTC wasn't swayed by either appeal and signed off on the CME's decision. The prevailing view among regulators at the time was that Libor couldn't be manipulated. Since the top and bottom quartile of quotes were discarded, they believed it would be almost impossible to rig the rate without mass collusion. They also thought that banks would be discouraged from even attempting to game the system since the firms' individual submissions were published at midday for everyone to see. Anyone who started inputting dubious figures, the logic went, would instantly be identified by their peers and held to account.

In reality, manipulating Libor was a lot easier than anybody had thought. What authorities around the world failed to recognize was that even lenders that made submissions too high or too low to be included in the final calculation could still influence where Libor was set because they pushed a previously excluded rate back into the pack.[9] Traders with vast derivatives positions only needed to move the rate by a few hundredths of a percentage point to make huge profits, and their influence was small enough to evade detection. On a $100 billion portfolio of interest-rate swaps, a bank could gain millions of dollars from a 1 basis point move.

Where Libor is set not only affects how much money banks and other sophisticated investors make on their derivatives bets, it also dictates how much interest U.S. homeowners pay on their mortgages each month. And poorer people with bad credit profiles are disproportionately affected. In Ohio, for example, 90 percent of all subprime mortgages in 2008 were indexed to Libor, double the proportion for prime loans.[10]

From his sitting room in Kalyves, Zombanakis can see the house where he grew up. He says he sometimes struggles to recognize the modern world of investment banking, where traders take home multimillion-pound bonuses and cheat their clients at the drop of a hat. He counts Farmanfarmaian, and many of his other clients, as lifelong friends. "Back then the market was small and run by a few gentlemen," Zombanakis says. "We took it for granted that gentlemen wouldn't try to manipulate things like that. But as the market was getting bigger, you couldn't trust it. You couldn't control it. Banking now is like a prostitution racket run by pimps. There's just too much money involved."

Chapter 4

A Day in the Life

Hayes may have been predisposed to fixate on financial markets, but he was also a product of his environment. And to be a trader is to have an addiction. He wakes no later than dawn and immediately reaches for his smartphone to find out what's happened in the market while he was asleep. His journey into the office is spent absorbing data until his brain is saturated. By the time he gets to his desk, he has already taken in a mass of information filtered on the basis of its usefulness in predicting movements in short-term interest rates: economic reports, news articles, e-mails, prices. He scans them quickly and moves on to the next item. If he's lucky, a trading strategy crystallizes in his mind.

After nodding towards his colleagues, he pulls on his headset and begins calling his brokers. The next eight hours are spent in a state of heightened focus amid the frenzy. He never stops talking, listening, typing, reacting. In the rare moments he's not offering prices or closing deals, he's working on improving the accuracy of the spreadsheets he uses to help spot price anomalies and identify opportunities. It's utterly immersive. There are no meetings during the trading day and no lunch break. The only reprieve is a five-minute run to the toilet or the bank's in-house coffee bar. His pulse is elevated. His pupils dilate. The room erupts every time an unexpected announcement hits the newswires. The levels of cortisol, serotonin and testosterone in his system spike, then fall away as his profits ebb and flow.

All his interactions are with brokers, traders or co-workers. They speak the same language he does. Their messages are crude, chummy, concise. Everyone has a nickname. Words are dropped in sentences and vowels are cut from messages to save time. A billion dollars changes hands with seven keystrokes. He has hundreds of conversations a day and almost all of them are over within 20 seconds. He works two feet from his colleagues and he couldn't tell you the color of their eyes. There is no time for small talk. Get the information, seal the deal, move on.

By the time the market closes, he's spent. But he still has meetings to go to and admin to complete before he can think about leaving. Once a year he attends a compulsory compliance class. It has nothing to do with his job. If he's busy, his boss—the best, most ruthless trader—will simply excuse him. He signs an online compliance manual he hasn't read or gets a junior to do it. Hayes goes to bars and restaurants a couple of times a month with counterparts at other firms, courtesy of the brokers who laugh at their jokes and pick up the tab. Most traders are out much more frequently. Over time he comes to regard them as friends as well as peers. They understand his life, think the same way as he does. Their seven-figure incomes set them apart from family and friends. No matter how raucous, their conversation always comes back to the market.

Most nights he'll head home. He tries to relax, but it's impossible when he knows that at any minute a sudden shift in prices could cost him millions. His main market may be closed, but his book is live 24 hours a day, rising and falling with movements in other countries. He checks his smartphone incessantly. His perspective has become myopically short term. He struggles to hold a conversation or follow the TV show he's put on before heading to bed. He hasn't read a novel from cover to cover in years. He wakes up during the night. It's dawn again. He checks his phone. His life is on a loop.

On weekends he finds it hard to unwind. He is impatient, disengaged. At dinner parties, people think he's rude and arrogant. He doesn't understand why they take so long to get to the point. If he can, he'll sleep till noon. His holidays are canceled or cut short at the last minute. In winter he's invited on broker-funded ski trips with the dozen or so traders in his market. In summer it's Las Vegas. In between there are motorsport days, boat trips, horse racing. They work so hard, they deserve it, he reasons. But still, he's stressed. He finds it hard to stay healthy. His colds last longer than they should and he can't shake injuries. Finding time to exercise or schedule a doctor's appointment is a problem. His colleagues drink and smoke too much. The temptation of drugs is always there. He tries to ignore the accelerated signs of aging. His relationships suffer. How do you explain to somebody outside the industry how it feels to lose $5 million in a single trade? Or why his £1 million bonus was insultingly low after the year he's had?

Somewhere along the way, his belief system gets subsumed by that of the company he keeps. The decisions he makes become indistinguishable from those of his firm and his peers. His priorities shift. Moral considerations are subjugated. His laser focus is on accumulating money and avoiding losses: That alone is what determines the size of his bonus; that is what confers his status in the world. He is a trader. It is his profession and his hobby, his social life and his identity. There is no room for anything else.

■ ■ ■

Hayes's job was to make his employer as much money as possible buying and selling derivatives. How exactly he did that—the special concoction of strategies, skills and tricks that make up a trader's DNA—was largely left up to him. First and foremost he was a market maker, providing liquidity to his clients, who were mostly traders at other banks. From the minute he logged onto his Bloomberg terminal and the red light next to his name turned green, Hayes was on the phone quoting guaranteed bid and offer prices on the vast inventory of products he traded. Hayes prided himself on always being open for business no matter how choppy the markets.[1] It was his calling card.

Hayes likened this part of his job to owning a fruit and vegetable stall. Buy low, sell high and pocket the difference. But rather than apples and pears, he dealt in complex financial securities worth hundreds of millions of dollars. His profit came from the spread between how much he paid for a security and how much he sold it for. In volatile times, the spread widened, reflecting the increased risk that the market might move against him before he had the chance to trade out of his position.

Making markets offered a steady stream of income, but it wasn't where the big money came from.

The thing that really set Hayes apart was his ability to spot price anomalies and exploit them, a technique known as relative value trading. It appealed to his lifelong passion for seeking out patterns—a classic Asperger's trait. During quiet spells, he spent his time scouring data, hunting for unseen opportunities. If he thought that the price of two similar securities had diverged unduly, he would buy one and short the other, betting that the spread between the two would shrink.

Every time Hayes entered a trade, his trading book shifted slightly. Imagine it's Jan. 1 and Hayes is sitting at his desk pondering whether short-term interest rates will rise or fall. The Japanese economy is improving, the Bank of Japan has made some noises about raising the base rate and Hayes reasons that they'll probably go up. He calls his broker, who goes into the market to find someone willing to take the other side of the trade.

Minutes later his broker comes back with a counterparty: a trader at another bank who is convinced that rates will fall. After thrashing out the details, the two traders agree to enter a three-year swap. Under the terms of this hypothetical deal, every six months for three years Hayes will pay a fixed rate of interest on a given sum—let's say 1 billion yen (£7.3 million)—and receive a variable amount from the trader at the other bank—let's say whatever six-month yen Libor is on those days. Let's assume that six-month Libor on the day of the deal is 1 percent, and the fixed interest rate Hayes agrees to pay out is also 1 percent.

Hayes now has a vested interest in Libor being as high as possible on the days the contract fixes every six months. On July 1, the first such day, Hayes will pay his counterparty the flat rate of 1 percent on the 1 billion yen, or 10 million yen. However, if his instincts were correct and six-month Libor has gone up to, say, 1.10 percent, he will receive 11 million yen from the other trader, pocketing a 1 million yen profit. On every trade there is a winner and a loser.

Now consider that Hayes is entering dozens of swaps and other similar deals each day. Before long he has fixes every day. Sometimes he may want the three-month rate to go up and the six-month rate to fall. Other times he might want them all to move higher. Some days his fixes are small, others they are huge. Part of the skill when pushing Libor around was knowing when to sacrifice a small gain for a big one coming down the track.

In every currency there were Libor rates for 15 durations: overnight, one week, two weeks, one month, and then monthly up to a year. The ones that really mattered to Hayes were the daily three-month and six-month yen Libors, because they featured most widely in the instruments he traded.

Everywhere he worked, Hayes set up his software to tell him exactly how much he stood to gain or lose from every fraction of a move in Libor in each currency and maturity. On any given day he would know what impact, say, a 1 basis point rise in three-month Libor and a quarter of a point fall in six-month Libor would have on his profit and loss, or P&L.

One of Hayes's favorite trades involved betting that the gap between Libor in different durations would widen or narrow: what's known in the industry as a basis trade. For example, Hayes may think, based on historic market patterns, that three-month yen Libor is cheap relative to the six-month rate and take a position. He also liked to bet on the spread between different benchmarks, such as three-month yen Libor and three-month Tibor. The Tokyo interbank offered rate was similar to Libor, but while the majority of banks on the Libor panel were Western, Tibor was based on estimates mostly from Japanese lenders.

Each time Hayes made a trade, he would have to decide whether to lay off some of his risk by hedging his position using, for example, other derivatives.[1] With scores of instruments, currencies and benchmarks, the possibilities were practically limitless.

All of this dealing created a constantly changing tradebook stretching years into the future, which was mapped out on a vast Excel spreadsheet. Hayes liked to think of it as a living organism with thousands of interconnected moving parts. In a corner of one of his screens was a number he looked at more than any other: his rolling P&L. Ask any trader worth his salt and he'll be able to give it to you to the nearest $1,000. It was Hayes's self-worth boiled down into a single indisputable number.

Chapter 5

Buy the Cash Boys
a Curry!

Hayes closed his eyes, took a breath and let the sound of the trading floor wash over him. It was October 2006 and he was fuming. He'd touched down in Japan more than two months ago, but a complication with his visa had prohibited him from placing a single trade. For weeks he'd felt like a substitute warming up the bench during a big game. Now that he'd finally been let loose he was already on the losing side of a huge bet on the direction of short-term interest rates.[1] Yen Libor was refusing to budge, and he was getting angrier. He loved his job, but when things weren't going his way he hated it just as much.

Hayes's desk was one of hundreds set out in a matrix on the fifth floor of UBS's Tokyo headquarters in a pair of identical white skyscrapers facing each other across a busy square. Curving like a shield in front of him were screens that beamed into his eyeballs the universe of prices, newsfeeds and trading interfaces he needed to stay on top of the ever-shifting markets. Below them was a squawk box covered in buttons that instantly connected him to his brokers and contacts in the market. Every few seconds a voice would come on the line offering him "10 yards of 2 year" or "lib tib at 34". Everything was set up to maximize speed and minimize effort. He had two keyboards, flanked by a pair of lucky panda toys.

That morning he'd walked through his lucky turnstile. Hayes had lucky underwear, a lucky t-shirt and lucky pants.[2] None of it was working.

That afternoon, Hayes was venting about his predicament to one of his brokers in London when a light bulb lit up in his mind, he would later recall. Banks had tailored their Libor submissions to benefit their own positions for as long as he'd been in the business. If a trader needed a high six-month rate one morning, he would fire a message to the individual on his firm's cash desk responsible for setting Libors that day and ask him to nudge his submission up half a basis point. Still, the system resisted tampering. No single institution could have much impact on the overall rate when 15 other banks were doing the same thing, pulling in different directions; and even if traders occasionally asked their buddies at other banks for favors, the effect on the published rate was minimal.

But what if Hayes could get his brokers to lie to the banks about what was happening in the cash markets? Maybe some of the lazier rate-setters, those who didn't do much business in the currency anyway, would simply follow along. Through his brokers, Hayes realized, he could sway several submitters at once, pulling their strings without them even knowing it. And Hayes was on better terms with his brokers than most. The biggest yen derivatives traders were based in Tokyo and had few if any ties to London, where the rate was set. But Hayes knew the London market. He quickly grasped that those connections could be his edge over the competition.

Brokers are the middlemen in the world of finance, facilitating deals between traders at different banks in everything from Treasury bonds to over-the-counter derivatives. If a trader wants to buy or sell, he could theoretically ring all the banks to get a price. Or he could go through a broker who is in touch with everyone and can find a counterparty in seconds. Hardly a dollar changes hands in the cash and derivatives markets without a broker matching the deal and taking his cut.

In the opaque, over-the-counter derivatives market, where there is no centralized exchange, brokers are at the epicenter of information flow. That puts them in a powerful position. Only they can get a picture of what all the banks are doing. While brokers had no official role in setting Libor, the rate-setters at the banks relied on them for information on where cash was trading. That was especially true for yen since the traders were trying to come up with their numbers after Tokyo, the busiest yen market in the world, had closed. Deals in London, particularly for longer periods, were sporadic at best.

Though the relationship between trader and broker is symbiotic, they are far from equals. Brokers typically earn a modest salary compared with their clients, with the bulk of their pay determined by the commissions they generate. That gives high-volume traders like Hayes a lot of leverage. Hayes's peers looked down on brokers as their intellectual and social inferiors, giving them derogatory nicknames like Brick and Village, as in "thick as a brick" and "village idiot". The broker's job is simply to match buy and sell orders and doesn't require the same complex math skills as trading derivatives. Developing and maintaining long-term relationships with clients is far more important.

Hayes's genius was to spot that these middlemen, overlooked by many of his privately educated peers, were the key to controlling Libor. Broadly speaking, brokers can be divided into two camps. There are technical brokers, who understand their clients' trading books and are quick to put them into profitable trades. Hayes gave them business because they were useful allies in the market. Then there are relationship brokers, who don't have much technical understanding but have good contacts and ready access to information.

Hayes's best broker in London was Darrell Read, a tall, ramrod-straight ICAP veteran who was firmly in the technical camp. Politely spoken with neatly trimmed dark hair and thin lips, Read was more cerebral than many of his colleagues and often walked around with a book under his arm. At ICAP, where everyone has a nickname, he was known as Big Nose or Noggin. Unlike most of his workmates, Read had not only finished his schooling, attending Gravesend Grammar School in Kent, but also went on to get a degree in zoology and geography from the University of Liverpool. He was diverted from his planned career as a bank manager in 1987, when a director of City of London brokerage Godsell, Astley & Pearce, who Read knew from his local rugby club, offered him a job.

Whenever a trader leaves a bank, his replacement inherits his brokers. Hayes had inherited Read shortly after he joined RBS as a hungry but naive trainee.

Read looked out for the rookie trader and on several occasions intervened to prevent him making errors that would have cost his firm millions.³ Such loyalty was rare among brokers, and the pair had spoken almost every day since. Now in his forties, Read had a deep knowledge of the market and Hayes often asked his opinion on trading strategies. While Hayes treated some of his brokers as errand boys, he saw Read as an equal. The two were close friends, meeting up for a drink whenever Hayes was back in the U.K.

Traders may look down on brokers as second-class citizens, but in the hierarchy of interdealer broking ICAP is at the top of the tree. The firm, which employs about 5,000 people, was set up by the notoriously imperious former Conservative Party Treasurer Michael Spencer in 1986, just as markets took off. Spencer, a friend of former U.K. Prime Minister David Cameron, is in many ways the epitome of the British establishment. Each year ICAP holds a charity day where A-list celebrities and royalty take turns booking trades. Journalists are given tours of the trading floor, then schmoozed over expensive bottles of Barolo from Spencer's in-house wine collection. Even ICAP's plush London headquarters look more like an investment bank than a brokerage, its walls adorned with paintings by Jack Vettriano and L.S. Lowry.

While the ICAP brokers worked hard, they partied even harder. Every Thursday and Friday at 5 p.m. hordes of them decamped to the local wine bar Brasserie Roque—"Brasrock" to those in the know— where they mingled with gaggles of women who had traveled in from Essex in the hope of bagging a big-spending city boy. If a broker spotted a girl he fancied he'd shout "mine", broker-speak for this is my deal. Pints of lager and glasses of champagne were interspersed with regular trips to the toilets, where there was always a queue for the cubicles. They were a tribe, with their own vocabulary and dress code: loafers, preferably by Gucci, open-necked shirts with big collars and oversize watches.

Read shunned the broker lifestyle. He arrived at the office long after the rabble had headed off for the evening and worked through the night to service his clients in Tokyo. Part of his value to Hayes was as a conduit to Colin Goodman, the ICAP employee responsible for sending out an unofficial but closely monitored Libor prediction e-mail each morning.

Electronic communications that prosecutors subsequently unearthed appear to show Read cooperating with Hayes in moving the Libor rate for Hayes's benefit. Read, however, has always denied trying to influence Libor and says that the messages were designed to help Goodman make more accurate predictions since Hayes was such an influential figure in the market. When Read was tried in a London court in 2015, the jury accepted his account and acquitted him. ICAP paid a £54 million fine to U.S. and U.K. regulators in 2013 for helping Hayes rig Libor.[4]

Goodman's e-mail, titled "the run-thru", was supposed to be an impartial reflection of where cash was trading in the market. It was received by more than a hundred traders and brokers, including representatives from 13 of the 16 banks on the yen Libor panel. If Hayes could somehow influence it, he realized, he would have a real shot at taming Libor once and for all.

Shortly after Hayes started at UBS, Read had told him he had gone to school with a trader at one of the rate-setting banks, Germany's WestLB—a firm that barely traded derivatives and had little financial interest in where Libor ended up.[5] On Oct. 18, 2006, Hayes was scanning his screens for the numbers that the yen panel banks had submitted the previous day, when he spotted that WestLB had input one of the lowest rates. He had a huge position about to mature, and every increase of a hundredth of a percentage point was worth hundreds of thousands of dollars. He pulled forward his keyboard and tapped out a quick instant message to Read.

"Hi mate, can you get your mate at WestLB to put 6m libor up! He has it at .51!" Hayes wrote. The published rate the previous day had been 0.524, so WestLB was near the bottom of the pack.

Read's buddy had been off work for the past week, the broker told Hayes. "NOT SURE WHEN BACK."

"OK lets hope its before next weds i have 350b 6m fix then!" Hayes replied, indicating he had 350 billion yen—about £2 billion—fixing off that day's six-month rate.

"GOTCHA," said Read.[6]

WestLB's six-month submission jumped four basis points that day. Two days later, Read sent an e-mail to Goodman asking: "Can u please get 3mos and 6mos as high as is possible today please…will sort you out a curry."

Goodman, a slight, quiet man, had interviewed Read at Godsells, which was later acquired by ICAP, when he'd come in for that first broking job two decades earlier, and the two men had developed a close, easy relationship. These days they worked in different areas within the firm. Read brokered yen derivatives, while Goodman was a yen cash broker, buying and selling short-term loans in the so-called money markets.

Goodman had been sending out his daily yen run-through since the mid-1990s and was now so well regarded in the cash markets that his colleagues called him Lord Libor, a moniker he relished, signing off his e-mails "M'Lord". Goodman increased his forecast and for the fourth consecutive day six-month yen Libor rose.

"thx for 6m Libor," Hayes wrote to Read on Oct. 23.

"no probs mate, got to buy the cash boys a curry this week!" he replied.

"i should buy it for them," Hayes told him.

"I'll let Michael Spencer do the honors," Read quipped.

To Hayes's mind, Libor was not only easy to manipulate but also cheap. He believed he had won Goodman's cooperation by dangling nothing more than a free takeaway. When Goodman was tried in 2015, he said his e-mail predictions only ever reflected his honest opinion, that he never expected banks to follow his predictions and that he found requests from others to move his predictions either up or down "annoying". He acknowledged sometimes agreeing to amend his e-mail but says he never actually did. He was acquitted by a jury.

Satisfied that the scheme was working with ICAP, Hayes decided to branch out. Terry Farr was the quintessential relationship broker. Loud and gregarious, with broad shoulders and a mop of blond hair, he more closely resembled a surfer than a banker. In the summer, he turned up at RP Martin's office dressed in shorts, flip-flops and aviator shades. He loved motorbikes and had a big tattoo plastered across one arm. Fun, friendly and quick-witted, "Tel" could often be found after work at The Hatchet, the pub a stone's throw from the office that acted as the firm's unofficial clubhouse. He lived with his wife and son in a small, end-of-terrace house on a busy road in Great Wakering, Essex. It was a far cry from the homes his clients owned in Notting Hill and Chelsea, but he was proud of his achievements. Farr had left school at 15, and his first job was helping his father out at a market stall selling flowers. He became a father young and had been forced to grow up fast.

Farr's knowledge of the derivatives market was minimal, but he knew everybody worth knowing, including many of the junior employees who input their banks' Libor rates each morning. People warmed to him and, if it didn't hurt their own positions, were happy to do him a favor. When Hayes asked Farr to lean on his bank contacts to change their submissions, he readily agreed. If Read contributed brains to Hayes's burgeoning operation, Farr provided the personality.

Farr later admitted helping Hayes move Libor, but was acquitted along with Read and Goodman. He told the court that he didn't know he wasn't allowed to influence the rate-setters and therefore hadn't acted dishonestly, an explanation accepted by the jury. Farr said he didn't understand how Libor was set or how a swap worked, claiming he didn't need to.

"I was known pretty much throughout my career as a relationship broker," Farr recalled on the stand. "Basically go out down the pub and have a few drinks, and something to eat. Or go to a sporting event, something like that. I was pretty good at that."[7]

Led by David Caplin, an eccentric old-school banker known as Mustard, RP Martin was a throwback to how trading was done in the 1970s. With fewer than 200 employees, there was no training or compliance oversight to speak of, and staff were remunerated and promoted based primarily on the commissions they brought in.[8] Caplin seemed to run the firm more like a club than a commercial enterprise. When the U.K. government banned smoking in the workplace, he spent £50,000 installing a balcony on the side of the building so Farr and his colleagues could slip out for a smoke.

Caplin knew he couldn't match the salaries paid by his bigger rivals, so he motivated his workers by offering them a 30 percent cut of the fees they earned. Long-standing employees were also given equity in the company.[9]

Over the following months, Hayes's days in Tokyo evolved into a familiar routine. From 7:30 a.m. to mid-afternoon he spent his time making markets and fine-tuning his longer-term trading strategies. Then, at 3:30 p.m., when the brokers in London logged on, his focus turned to Libor. Hayes bombarded Read and Farr with hundreds of IMs, e-mails and phone calls asking for help moving Libor. It was a relentless barrage of short, sharp instructions for what he needed that day: "higher 6m", "lower 3m", "low 1m". Read passed the messages on to Goodman in e-mails that began "morning begging email!!!!" and "On the scrounge again." Farr approached his friends at banks and asked them to nudge their Libor figures as "a small favour" or a "personal favour".

Read, Goodman and Farr were all found not guilty of conspiring to defraud. In their 2015 trial, they produced evidence that they said showed them defying Hayes's requests and misleading the trader about the extent of their assistance. In one e-mail, dated Oct. 23, 2008, Read told Goodman to avoid sending Hayes the run-thru because he sometimes lied about his influence on the forecast. "I lie about the levels all the time and it makes my life easier," Read wrote. Goodman's lawyers cited several occasions when the broker told Read he would adjust his forecast to appease Hayes but in fact never did.

Hayes may have felt a closer affinity to his brokers than to many of his colleagues, but he regularly reprimanded them if he believed they weren't working hard enough for him. His favorite trick was threatening he would "pull their line"—stop doing business with them—if they didn't up their game. After shouting and screaming at them, he sometimes acted as though nothing had happened when they spoke again the following day.

Hayes's business was conducted on a Bloomberg terminal, the ubiquitous trading system whose black and amber interface can be seen in the background of just about every Wall Street movie. The system has a dedicated page showing what each of the 16 banks had submitted to yen Libor for every duration. Before long Hayes was consulting it daily, obsessively tracking what each firm submitted.

If Hayes had a large position, he would tell Farr to target specific individuals whose inputs were having a disproportionate impact on the overall rate. If Farr didn't have a contact at a particular bank, Hayes would ask him to offer fictitious bids, known as "spoof offers", to the rate-setter over the squawk box in the hope that it might influence his thinking.[10] Hayes encouraged Farr to make new contacts, offering to pick up the tab for any entertainment that might be needed to seal the deal.

Later, many in the industry questioned how much impact Hayes could have on the published rate since he was only ever able to influence a handful of banks. However, what Hayes was aiming for was momentum. If three submitters from prominent banks consistently input low rates over the course of a few days, other contributors would start to follow suit, assuming that their rivals had a better read of the cash markets. If everything went according to plan, before long the rate might have moved several basis points, all thanks to Hayes and his tinkering.

Hayes was quickly becoming one of the biggest and most aggressive traders in the yen market, putting hundreds of millions of dollars of trades a week through Read and Farr. The brokers stood to earn substantial commissions, and they owed it all to Hayes. As he told them repeatedly: "If I make money, so do you."[11]

Believing that the brokers were now squared away and doing his bidding, Hayes started looking closer to home for assistance. UBS's markets business was split on two main lines: the investment bank, where traders like Hayes resided and which brought in all the profit, and the cash or treasury business, which made sure the bank had enough money to fund its various outgoings. The cash department was considered unglamorous—an essential but dull activity that kept the business afloat so that the superstars could work their magic. It attracted more dependable, less aggressive types looking to build a career—individuals who were content to take home a fraction of what the traders earned in exchange for job security and a less stressful existence. Cash traders spent their days borrowing and lending for short periods in the money markets, and were skilled at gauging how much interest UBS would be charged. They were therefore the obvious candidates to set Libor. The hub of the cash business was in UBS's global headquarters in Zurich. It was there that, each morning, the majority of Libor rates were input onto an online system by a handful of employees who were, to Hayes's mind, "grunts".[12]

When Hayes had arrived in Tokyo, he was amazed that none of the derivatives traders on his desk seemed to ask UBS's rate-setters for help. It was standard practice at RBS. If he was going to have a shot at controlling Libor, it was only logical to get the submitters at his own bank on board, automatically shoring up one of the 16 contributing banks. But while the rates were physically input in Zurich, it was a mid-level manager on UBS's short-term interest-rate trading desk in Singapore named Roger Darin who made the final decision.

Unfortunately for Hayes, he and Darin had history. There was bad blood between the pair dating back to Hayes's time at RBC, when they were sometimes counterparties on the same deals. On one occasion

Hayes had become angry when he thought UBS had submitted a six-month rate designed solely to boost the profitability of the Swiss bank's positions, he would later tell investigators. To test the theory, Hayes said he got one of RBC's cash traders to call Darin and ask him how much interest the bank would charge RBC to borrow cash for six months. When the price he quoted was out of line with the Libor rate they'd just submitted, the trader threatened to report Darin to the BBA.[13]

On Nov. 14, Hayes sent Darin an unusually polite instant message. "Hi Roger who sets our Libors."

"me," came the reply. "(or the guy in Zurich.) we use the cash to derive them."

"ok cld really do w 6m up pls if poss," Hayes asked.

"so tend to accurately reflect the movements," Darin replied, emphasizing that Libor was supposed to be independent.

"Then I needn't worry :)," Hayes wrote.

"We been on the high side for a while," Darin said. "Will give it an extra notch today."

Short, tubby and cross-eyed, Darin had been climbing the greasy pole at UBS for more than two decades, starting out in Zurich in a clerical position and working his way up. During that time he'd seen big shots like Hayes come and go. Darin's main job was to trade short-term loans to fund the bank's balance sheet and hopefully earn a profit in the process. He had a modest trading book, which rose and fell with each day's Libors and made markets in some of the same instruments as Hayes. For years, e-mails suggest, he'd been skewing the bank's Libors. At UBS, as at many banks, it was part of the job. Darin, whose case is making its way through the U.S. courts, refutes the charges. He argues he was told by UBS's managers to comply with Hayes's requests and frequently pushed back.

Now that Darin seemed to be willing, it was difficult to close the floodgates. Two days later Hayes was back in touch, asking for another high six-month rate. This time Darin had a position the other way round.

"If I take that off your hands then you can set higher?" Hayes asked. He was proposing that Darin trade out of his smaller position by doing a separate trade with Hayes, so he no longer stood to lose if the rate went up.

"Sounds fair," Darin replied. E-mails produced during Hayes's trial suggest it was an arrangement they would repeat.

While they remained outwardly civil in the months ahead, the animosity between them was never far below the surface. Darin was UBS's yen Libor gatekeeper, the one individual who stood in the way of Hayes's quest for absolute control, and Hayes resented him bitterly for it.

Hayes's claim to be able to influence Libor didn't go unnoticed in Tokyo. Everyone on the desk had his or her own trading book whose value also depended on where Libor set. Soon, he was given responsibility for handling the whole team's exposure to the benchmark, Hayes would later testify. At regular morning meetings he discussed his positions and explained to his bosses and colleagues how he planned to influence the rate that day.[14] What had started out as one man's sporadic enterprise was morphing into something much more organized.

The brokers may have been useful conduits to the rest of the market, but sometimes, Hayes realized, he could cut out the middlemen. He still knew some of the individuals who set their bank's Libors from his London days, and early in 2007 he began to approach them directly. In the world of trading, everyone needs a friend and favors are dished out readily—you never know when you might need one back. Hayes's network included Will Hall, who was in the same graduate trainee program at RBS and who had taken over Hayes's job when he left for RBC. Hall was close to Paul White, the RBS rate-setter, and stepped in for him when he was away. On June 28, 2007, Hayes wrote to his former colleague: "Can you ask for a high 6m Libor today?" Seconds later, Hall replied that he would try, although there's no evidence that he passed the request on. Hayes knew Hall was unhappy at RBS and promised to put in a good word for him with his bosses at UBS. He never did.[15]

Hayes's lack of social graces and brusque nature should have meant opportunities to pull in favors were limited, but he was such a high-volume trader that rivals at other banks didn't want to get on his wrong side. When Hayes reached out to Stuart Wiley, a young JPMorgan Chase trader he'd met at social events, and asked him to lean on the U.S. bank's submitters, Wiley wrote back: "I will try my best." Privately, Wiley, who was never charged with a crime, complained that Hayes was crazy.[16]

Around the same time, Hayes's stepbrother returned to London after a short stint with HSBC in New York. Peter O'Leary was a graduate trainee several years younger than Hayes. Though not biologically related—Hayes's mother had married O'Leary's father—the two had grown up under the same roof and were close. When chatting with friends, Hayes referred to O'Leary simply as his brother. One afternoon in April 2007, O'Leary sent Hayes an e-mail asking how he was getting on. Hayes sensed an opportunity. HSBC was one of the banks on the yen Libor panel and, so far, Hayes hadn't had much luck influencing it. After some small talk about a mutual friend's wedding, Hayes asked: "Do you know the guy who sets yen Libors at your place? I think he trades yen and scandi cash and his name is Chris Darcy."

"Ha ha yeah I do!" O'Leary replied. "His name is actually Chris Porter I think. Everyone calls him Darcy, I think, because he sounds pretty posh."

"Mate, can you do me a huge favor and ask him if he will set his three-month yen Libor on the low side for the next few days as I have $1 million of fixes?" Hayes typed. "It would be a massive help if you can. If you can't, don't worry."

It was an audacious request. Not only was O'Leary about as junior as it gets, but he didn't trade derivatives and had no idea how Libor was set. O'Leary promised to try, but as it edged closer to 11 a.m. in London, the deadline for submitting Libor, Hayes still hadn't heard back from him. He dialed his work number.

"He's going to set his Libors in the next 10 minutes mate," Hayes reminded him. "Do you know him well?"

After initially promising to help, O'Leary had become reluctant. Porter worked on a different floor, in a different part of the business, he told Hayes. In fact, he didn't think Porter even knew his name— he had accidentally called him Patrick the last time they'd bumped into each other. Hayes persisted, coaching his stepbrother on how to make the approach, suggesting he befriend him over a few beers. Tommy Chocolate, the nervy oddball with the superhero duvet, had come a long way.

"I thought, oh well, if Peter knows him he might be able to ask as a favor, just to set it on the low side for the next, you know, few days," Hayes reasoned aloud to his brother, keeping his tone light-hearted. "I don't know how well you know him but if you get to know him better it would be a big help for me."

Eventually O'Leary relented and agreed to relay the request.[17] Later that day, Hayes rang him again.

"Just say, if you can set a low yen three-month Libor it would really help my brother out," Hayes told him, prompting O'Leary to laugh nervously. "Seriously mate," Hayes continued, undeterred. "I've got like a fucking million bucks fixes."

Hayes went back to O'Leary several more times over the next few weeks with similar requests. Eventually, in late June, Hayes had a change of heart. It was one thing leaning on brokers and fellow traders, but this was a step too far. In a rare moment of contrition, he called his brother, who was never charged, and apologized for dragging him into the scheme. It wasn't a huge concession: Hayes had noticed with some irritation that Porter was ignoring O'Leary's requests anyway.

By now, Hayes was making so much money he could afford to be magnanimous. He'd met ICAP's Lord Libor, Colin Goodman, for a drink on a flying visit to London and suggested setting up a way to reward him that was more appealing than the occasional curry.[18] Hayes lobbied his bosses to pay the broker a regular retainer. On top of the fixed monthly fee of about £70,000 that UBS paid ICAP for its services, Hayes arranged for an additional £15,000 a month, £5,000 of which was personally earmarked for Goodman. Hayes later told prosecutors that the money was for help influencing Libor, but during his trial Goodman denied the payments were a reward for skewing his prediction e-mail. He said it was Hayes's way to thank him for his knowledge of the cash market.

RP Martin was a much smaller outfit than ICAP, and UBS paid the firm by the trade rather than through a fixed monthly fee. The commission was uncapped, which meant Hayes could throw big trades Farr's way as incentive for his help on Libor. Farr, who later successfully argued he didn't know he was doing anything wrong, was more than happy with the arrangement: He often earned more in one trade with Hayes than he did in a whole week with other clients.

Hayes was becoming a monster, trading higher volumes than most of his competitors combined and bringing in profits once considered impossible in his market. The commission he paid ICAP alone was big enough that shortly after Hayes joined UBS, Read agreed to drop all his other clients to be available to him full time. In April 2007, after years on the graveyard shift, the broker moved to New Zealand with his wife and their two sons. Read hoped it would be a new start for the family he saw so little of in the U.K. They bought a house in Wellington, near a small ICAP office where Read could be on call for Hayes from 10 a.m. to 10 p.m.

For all his industry, Hayes never knew for certain how much influence he had on Libor. Often the rate would move in the direction he wanted, but there was no way of knowing if that was because of his efforts or blind chance. During their 2016 trial, several of the brokers accused of helping Hayes said they only ever fobbed him off. But if he couldn't quite control the future, he could give it a shove in whatever direction he wanted. Hayes later estimated that his ability to move the rate accounted for perhaps five or ten percent of his profits. It was enough. In the cutthroat world of trading, it was an edge over his competitors that helped mark him as a star at UBS and make $50 million for the bank in 2007.

That December, at a swimming pool on the roof of an expensive Tokyo hotel, he met Sarah Tighe, a tall, blonde corporate lawyer with blue eyes and a warm smile. Tighe was in Japan on vacation after completing her training contract at Shearman & Sterling in London. Like Hayes, she worked long hours in a challenging, stressful environment that left little room for anything else. In the days that followed, Hayes couldn't get Tighe out of his mind.[19] Outwardly serene, she had a fiery streak and an inner confidence. They agreed to meet again. This time she listened to him ramble on about the fortune he made off the collapse of Northern Rock bank and didn't glaze over. Tighe came from a family of Aston Villa fanatics and knew the intricacies of the British soccer leagues. She was a keeper, someone who found his idiosyncrasies endearing and his ambition attractive. When it was time for Tighe to return to London, they embarked on a long-distance relationship. She applied for jobs in Tokyo and, in May 2008, flew back to take up a position with Herbert Smith. They found a flat and moved in together straight away. Out of the chaos of markets and everyday life, Hayes was creating the order he so craved.

Chapter 6

Anything With
Four Legs

On an unseasonably cold April morning in 2008, Vince Mc-
Gonagle walked through the revolving doors at the Commodity Futures Trading Commission (CFTC), a modern orange-
brick building on a quiet street in Washington. He placed his wallet,
glasses and raincoat in a gray tray and walked slowly through the security scanner. After collecting his belongings, McGonagle turned left at
the end of the lobby and caught an elevator to the seventh floor, just like
he did every day.

Small and wiry with a hangdog expression, McGonagle had been at
the enforcement division of the CFTC for 11 years, during which time
his red hair had turned gray around the edges. A practicing Catholic,
McGonagle got his law degree from Pepperdine University, a Christian
school in Malibu, California, where students are prepared for "lives of
purpose, service and leadership". While his classmates took highly paid
positions defending companies and individuals accused of corporate corruption, McGonagle opted to build a career bringing cases against them.
He joined the agency as a trial attorney and was now, at 44, a manager
overseeing teams of lawyers and investigators.

McGonagle closed the door to his office and settled down to read
the daily newspaper clippings e-mail. The CFTC, like all enforcement

agencies, relies on the press for tips on potential financial malfeasance. It was April 16, 2008, and the headline on page one of *The Wall Street Journal* read: "Bankers Cast Doubt on Key Rate Amid Crisis". It began:

> One of the most important barometers of the world's financial health could be sending false signals. In a development that has implications for borrowers everywhere, from Russian oil producers to homeowners in Detroit, bankers and traders are expressing concerns that the London interbank offered rate, known as Libor, is becoming unreliable.

The story, written at the *Journal's* London office near Fleet Street, went on to suggest that some of the world's largest banks might have been providing deliberately low estimates of their borrowing costs to avoid tipping off the market "that they're desperate for cash". That was having the effect of distorting Libor, and therefore trillions of dollars of securities around the world.

The article's author was Carrick Mollenkamp, a veteran business reporter from the Deep South who had been detailed to London to cover the financial crisis. Mollenkamp's sources told him that banks were paying much more for cash than they were letting on.[1] They feared if they were honest they could go the same way as Bear Stearns, the 85-year-old New York securities firm that had collapsed the previous month.

The big flaw in Libor was that it relied on banks to tell the truth but encouraged them to lie. When the 150 variants of the benchmark were released each day, the banks' individual submissions were also published, giving the world a snapshot of their relative creditworthiness. Historically, the individuals responsible for making their firm's Libor submissions were able to base their estimates on a vibrant interbank money market, in which banks borrowed cash from each other to fund their day-to-day operations. They were prevented from deviating too far from the truth because their fellow market participants knew what rates they were really being charged. Over the previous few months, that had changed. Banks had stopped lending to each other for periods of longer than a few days, preferring to stockpile their cash. After Bear Stearns there was no guarantee they would get it back.

With so much at stake, lenders had become fixated on what their rivals were inputting. Any outlier at the higher—that is, riskier—end was in danger of becoming a pariah, unable to access the liquidity it needed to fund its balance sheet. Soon banks began to submit rates they thought would place them in the middle of the pack rather than what they truly believed they could borrow unsecured cash for. The motivation for lowballing was not tied to profit—many banks actually stood to lose out from lower Libors. This was about survival.

Ironically, just as Libor's accuracy faltered, its importance rocketed. As the financial crisis deepened, central bankers monitored Libor in different currencies to see how successful their latest policy announcements were in calming markets. Governments looked at individual firms' submissions for clues as to who they might be forced to bail out next. If banks were lying about Libor, it was not just affecting interest rates and derivatives payments. It was skewing reality.

McGonagle stood up and walked to the window of his office, which sat in the southwest corner of the Lafayette Centre, a short walk from the Cathedral of St. Matthew the Apostle. He had heard of Libor before— as the benchmark used to calculate the floating leg in swaps contracts. But, for now at least, the over-the-counter swaps market fell outside the CFTC's reach.

Still, the story struck a chord. Shortly after joining the agency, McGonagle had been part of a team of enforcement lawyers appointed to investigate Texas energy company Dynegy over allegations it had lied about how much natural gas it was buying and selling in order to influence benchmarks used to set prices in the commodity.

McGonagle's team had been sent to Houston to interview traders at the firm. In natural gas markets, benchmark prices are compiled and published daily by private companies like Platts and Argus, which call traders at the biggest market participants and ask them about the trades they have undertaken that day. Their responses are averaged to produce a benchmark price, which is used as a guide to the going rate for gas around the world.

A week before Christmas 2002, Dynegy was fined $5 million for fabricating trades in order to influence the benchmark and boost the profitability of its gas futures positions. The relatively small fine reflected Dynegy's cooperation in helping the authorities build cases against its competitors, and over the next four years the CFTC, working with the Federal Energy Regulatory Commission and the Department of

Justice, dished out penalties totaling $300 million to more than two dozen energy firms across the U.S., including Enron and American Electric. Benchmark manipulation in energy markets was not just down to a few bad apples. It was an industrywide practice.

Around the same time, the newspaper industry was undergoing its own shakedown. Between 2003 and 2004, venerable publications including *Newsday*, the *Chicago Sun-Times* and *The Dallas Morning News* were ordered to compensate advertisers after artificially inflating circulation figures. The papers used elaborate schemes including delivering to nonexistent addresses and deceased customers to pump up the sales figures they provided to the Audit Bureau of Circulation by hundreds of thousands of copies a day.

"Everybody was false reporting," recalls Steve Obie, one of McGonagle's colleagues at the CFTC at the time and now an attorney in private practice. "Anytime there's human beings involved and there's the potential to make money, they do it. It was discussed at every industry event for a while. That's why it's so surprising nobody picked up on Libor."

There was no inkling at this stage that traders like Hayes were pushing Libor around to boost their profits, but the similarities to energy and newspaper fraud were striking: Here was a benchmark that relied on the honesty of traders who had a direct interest in where it was set. While natural gas benchmarks were compiled by private companies, Libor was overseen by the BBA, the London-based lobbying group with a reputation for being a cheerleader for banks. In both cases, the body responsible for overseeing the rate had no punitive powers, so there was little to discourage firms from cheating.

When McGonagle finished reading the *Journal* article, he e-mailed colleagues and asked them what they knew about Libor. That week he pulled aside Gretchen Lowe, one of the enforcement division's senior deputies, to get her take. Lowe was born in Chittenango, New York, not far from Syracuse. A straight-A student and gifted athlete, she was profiled in her local newspaper as a future star. She studied English and economics at the University of Rochester where, at close to six foot, she was a varsity volleyball player. Lowe joined the CFTC in 1995 after a few years working at a corporate law firm where she was bored stiff. Government work was less well paid, but to Lowe's mind more worthwhile. It was a trade-off she was willing to make. She'd worked with

McGonagle over the years and they had become staunch allies. In many ways they were alike. Serious, even austere, Lowe was naturally reserved, while McGonagle could clam up in social situations. They were often first into the office in the morning but nowhere to be seen if their colleagues were having a beer after work.

McGonagle's team put together a dossier about Libor, including some preliminary reports from within the financial community. In March, economists at the Bank for International Settlements, an umbrella group for central banks around the world, had published a paper that identified unusual patterns in Libor during the crisis, although it concluded these were "not caused by shortcomings in the design of the fixing mechanism".[2]

A month later, Scott Peng, an analyst at Citigroup in New York, sent his customers a research note that estimated the dollar Libor submissions of the 18 firms that set the rate were 20 to 30 basis points lower than they should have been because of a "prevailing fear" among the banks of "being perceived as a weak hand in this fragile market environment".[3]

While there was no evidence of manipulation by specific firms, McGonagle was coming around to the idea of launching an investigation. On a personal level, the timing was fortuitous. Rumors were making the rounds that the CFTC's head of enforcement, Greg Mocek, was leaving the agency. As No. 2 in Washington, McGonagle was his natural successor. But Obie, a well-connected, outwardly breezy attorney who ran enforcement in Manhattan, was also in the running.

Obie had joined the CFTC a year after McGonagle, and their careers had moved in tandem. Yet, despite working together on a number of cases, relations between the two were strained. A large man, Obie had a tendency to dominate discussions, causing McGonagle to shut down. Their contrasting personalities resulted in meetings in which the two either said nothing to each other or openly argued.[4] When McGonagle felt under pressure he had a habit of frantically taking notes, even when what was being discussed was of little consequence. He did that a lot when Obie was around.

Before law school, McGonagle had spent three years studying economics at La Salle University in Philadelphia. He funded his education by loading and unloading UPS trucks five nights a week. His friends in the blue-collar Tau Kappa Epsilon fraternity rarely saw him during the week because he was either studying or working, according to a former fraternity brother who remembers McGonagle as the only member of their group who wasn't given a nickname.

If the *Journal* report was right, Libor represented an opportunity for McGonagle to steal a march and stake ownership of a potentially huge case. McGonagle and Lowe both felt there was scope for further inquiry but wanted to confine their discussions to a small, trusted team until there was more to go on. They called another colleague, Anne Termine, and asked her to join them. Termine, a spirited and sometimes abrasive attorney, had started her career prosecuting drug dealers and murderers in the New Orleans District Attorney's Office before moving back to her native Washington in 2003. Stocky and little more than 5-foot-3 in heels, Termine stood in stark contrast to the older Lowe. She had made an impression at the CFTC by aggressively pursuing Atlanta, Georgia-based hedge fund Risk Capital, which was fined $22 million in 2006 for cold-calling investors and pressuring them into buying high-risk commodity options they didn't understand.

The three piled into McGonagle's office and, over the course of a few hours, hashed out a framework for an investigation into Libor. Termine would put together a small unit of attorneys and investigators to carry out initial discussions with people in the market: traders, academics, U.S. regulators and industry groups. Lowe agreed to oversee the case and liaise with other international agencies. The Office of the Chief Economist, the CFTC's in-house technical experts, was asked to carry out an analysis of movements in Libor in recent months. For McGonagle, the most pressing concern was getting support within the agency to pursue an investigation.

When the CFTC was formed in 1975, its raison d'être was to regulate a futures and options market dominated by farmers and corporations hedging exposures to fluctuations in commodity prices. In the intervening years, derivatives ballooned into a multitrillion-dollar industry spanning foreign exchange, equities and bonds, but the commission's stature had not grown commensurately.

While the agency had a broad remit to intervene in financial markets, it was still widely regarded as the wimpy younger brother of the regulatory community. Complex financial cases, matters of high finance and anything to do with governing Wall Street were automatically considered the preserve of the Securities and Exchange Commission, the Federal Reserve or the Office of the Comptroller of the Currency, all of which dwarfed the CFTC in terms of manpower and resources. As a civil body, it had no power to impose criminal sanctions on individuals or companies found guilty of wrongdoing.

The agency's place in the pecking order was reinforced by its structure and personnel. While the SEC is overseen by the powerful Senate Banking Committee, the CFTC answers to the Committee on Agriculture, Nutrition and Forestry. Its chairman and four commissioners are appointed by the president and have historically been drawn from rural areas and agricultural markets—"ag people" in Washington parlance.

According to one popular story in regulatory circles, Harvey Pitt, the SEC's notoriously gruff chairman from 2001 to 2003, was once discussing who had oversight of a particular product with a counterpart at the CFTC when he lost his patience and bellowed: "It's pretty simple. Anything that is a security or a financial instrument is ours. Anything that has four legs is yours."

CFTC rules dictate that any enforcement actions, such as launching an investigation or issuing subpoenas, need to be approved by the commissioners cloistered in plush offices on the ninth floor. In the spring of 2008 the agency was led by Walt Lukken, a lawyer in his forties who had been made acting chairman the previous summer. Lukken joined the CFTC in 2002 after a stint as counsel to the professional staff of the Senate agriculture committee and before that as an aide to Republican Senator Richard Lugar of Indiana, a state in the agricultural heartland of the American Midwest.

When Lukken was informed about the possibility of looking into Libor, his response was skeptical. If there were to be an investigation into the London interbank offered rate, it should be primarily the responsibility of the U.K. regulators. The clue was in the name. Besides, there was no evidence that the rate was being rigged and the suspicious movements in Libor in late 2007 had dissipated. Most importantly, the enforcement division was already badly overstretched.

Still, as a senior deputy, McGonagle had a degree of autonomy over which targets to aim for, and he didn't need sign-off from the commissioners to keep digging. Privately, he gave little credence to Lukken's concerns about jurisdiction. Under the Commodity Exchange Act, the CFTC had responsibility for trading in any commodity or futures contract that affects prices in interstate commerce, anywhere in the world. Interpreted broadly, the agency could go after Libor if it could be shown to have a direct impact on the markets it oversaw. Libor was also the benchmark for billions of dollars of interest-rate futures contracts traded on the Chicago Mercantile Exchange (CME), placing it squarely within the CFTC's purview.

While Termine and Lowe quietly gathered intelligence, the *Journal* was working on a follow-up that would help focus their minds. On May 29, 2008, the paper published a piece that compared movements in Libor since the start of the financial crisis with another barometer of stress: banks' credit default swaps prices.[5] CDS contracts are a type of financial derivative that allow investors to bet on the likelihood that an institution will default on its publicly traded debt. They are used by credit investors as a form of insurance but are also bought and sold by hedge funds and other financial speculators to take bets on a company's fortunes. Historically, Libor and CDS prices have moved in lockstep, rising during periods of stress. The *Journal* reported that in January, as fears grew about possible bank failures, the two measures started to diverge. While default insurance spiked, Libor saw only modest increases, supporting the theory that banks were not being honest about their predicament.

"What was really crazy, the fundamental statistical absurdity of it, was that you had all these banks with completely different credit situations all reporting the exact same rate every day," recalls Mark Whitehouse, a former *Journal* reporter and co-author of the article. "That looked patently wrong."

The *Journal* identified several institutions whose Libor submissions looked particularly out of whack with the cost of insuring their debt, including Citigroup and UBS. The same day, a senior Barclays banker in England broke ranks during a televised interview with Bloomberg and admitted his bank had felt forced into lowballing its submissions.

"We had one week in September where our treasurer, who takes his responsibilities pretty seriously, said: 'Right, I've had enough of this, I'm going to quote the right rates,'" said Tim Bond, head of asset-allocation research at Barclays at the time. "All we got for our pains was a series of media articles saying that we were having difficulty financing."

Bond was referring to the first week of September 2007, when Bloomberg published a column asking: "So what the hell is happening at Barclays and its Barclays Capital securities unit that is prompting its peers to charge it premium interest rates in the money market?"[6] That week the U.K. lender had posted three-month dollar rates as much as 8 basis points higher than the average of its peers. After the story appeared, the bank quietly lowered its submissions.

Bond articulated the dilemma banks were faced with: Be honest and risk having your head blown off, or lie and collectively skew the benchmark interest rate at the heart of the global financial system.

The CFTC's next step was to identify a manageable shortlist of firms to target. The focus was U.S. banks and those with a big presence in the country. The investigators picked five: Bank of America, Citigroup, JPMorgan, UBS and Barclays. That summer, Termine wrote to the banks requesting information on how the Libor-setting process worked. Because cooperation by the firms at that stage was voluntary, there was no need to get approval from the ninth floor. It was the first tentative step in what would become the biggest case of their lives.

Chapter 7

No One's Clean-Clean

Meanwhile, in the gray stone streets of the City of London, the guardians of Libor were panicking. The day the first *Journal* article was published, the British Bankers' Association was holding its annual meeting. Clouds gathered ominously overhead as senior executives from the world's biggest banks filed one by one into Pinners Hall, the trade association's neoclassical headquarters. They were supposed to be gathering to discuss the enveloping financial crisis. Allegations of Libor manipulation were an unwelcome distraction.

Since their last meeting the world had grown hostile and unrecognizable. Rising defaults on mortgages in the U.S. had spooked markets, drying up the easy flow of credit between financial institutions and exposing the shaky foundations upon which years of easy profits had rested. Banks were forced to write down the value of their assets by billions of dollars and were left perilously close to insolvency. Northern Rock was nationalized in February 2008 after the mortgage lender became the first British firm in 150 years to suffer a bank run. BNP Paribas, France's biggest lender, created panic the previous August when it froze redemptions from its funds, refusing to give investors their money back.

Most of the afternoon was spent discussing the pressing issue of how to access enough capital to stay alive. At one point, Angela Knight, the BBA's chief executive and a former politician, broached the issue of Libor. It's not acceptable for banks to be anything less than honest in their submissions, she reminded the group with a delivery reminiscent of Margaret Thatcher. Articles like the *Journal's* undermined the reputation of the industry, and any bank found to be lying about its borrowing costs could ultimately be removed from the panel, she added. The assembled chairmen and CEOs promised to pass on the message to their underlings.

Libor had been overseen by the BBA with little fanfare and few problems for two decades. Banks and other investors paid a fee to use the rate in financial contracts, which provided the BBA with a steady and significant stream of income.[1] Throughout that period Libor had been a source of pride as well as revenue. Now it was a major headache.

Ostensibly, the BBA's role was to police the banks to make sure that their submissions were accurate and fair. In an ideal world, when allegations like the *Journal's* were made, it would investigate and take whatever action was necessary to stamp out any funny business. The obvious flaw in the arrangement was that the group was hopelessly conflicted. The BBA's members were the same banks that sat on the Libor panels, banks whose annual subscriptions paid the BBA staff's wages.

There was also what could generously be called a skills gap. The BBA's Libor manager, John Ewan, was in his early thirties and had no banking experience. Prior to joining the association in 2005, he had spent time working in a call center before packing it in and traveling the world for 18 months. Tall and gawky with bulging eyes and prominent sideburns, Ewan frequently wore a startled expression. Behind his back, bosses fretted about whether he was up to the job.[2] During meetings he would sit quietly and take notes. He lacked the experience to stand up in a room full of veteran bankers and challenge their behavior. Much of what was being discussed, he later admitted, went straight over his head.[3]

It was an arrangement that suited the real nexus of power, the official-sounding Foreign Exchange and Money Markets Committee (FXMMC). The FXMMC was made up of about 15 representatives from Libor-setting banks who exercised a veto on anything Libor related. Ewan was there to act as secretariat. If a suggestion was made to the BBA for a way to reform the rate, it would ultimately need to be approved by the committee. Likewise, if evidence of manipulation was discovered, it was the committee that would decide on any punishment. In its 22-year history, not one firm had been sanctioned. The BBA brand was a fig leaf over a system in which poacher and gamekeeper were one and the same.

The way the group conducted its business was more akin to a meeting of the five families than a professional body. Members of the FXMMC were never named and no minutes of their meetings were published. They met every few months at undisclosed locations. All new members were proposed and then vetted by existing members. The BBA refused to divulge what was discussed or decided. For any journalists covering the markets, it was an information black hole.

Just before 5:30 p.m. on the evening of the meeting, Ewan got on the phone to Miles Storey, the FXMMC's chairman and a senior treasurer at Barclays, for a debriefing on the day's events. The two men spoke frequently. At the time, Barclays's submissions were more honest than most—maybe 10 basis points lower than where they should have been rather than 40 or 50.

"We're clean, but we're dirty clean rather than clean-clean," said Storey in a thick northern accent, summing up his frustration.

"No one's clean-clean now, are they Miles?" Ewan replied.[4]

News of Knight's threat to boot wayward banks off the panels had been reported by Bloomberg that afternoon. That's all well and good, said Storey, but any bank that unilaterally raised its rates now was liable to be massacred by the press and the markets. A solution had been hatched, Ewan reassured him.

"The idea is," Ewan said, to "see if we can gradually float the dollar rate slightly, gently up."

As it transpired they needn't have worried. The following morning, three-month dollar Libor jumped 8 basis points to 2.82 percent, its biggest rise in eight months. A day later the rate climbed 9 more basis points to 2.91 percent.[5] The threat of removal from the panels was enough to trigger what William Dudley, a Federal Reserve Bank of New York executive, described in a speech later that month as "an outbreak of veracity" among the banks.[6]

The media pounced on the moves as evidence of Libor's flaws with headlines like "Libor Credibility Questioned"[7] and "Libor Surges After Scrutiny Does".[8] Publicly, the BBA denied that the change in the banks' behavior had anything to do with fear of reprisals and went on what it described as a "charm offensive". In the weeks that followed, Ewan and Knight, immaculately dressed and sporting her trademark pearl necklace, conducted dozens of interviews with the world's media, at one stage inviting a group of reporters to the office where Libor submissions were vetted. For Ewan, who often complained about the press, it was a particularly galling experience. It's like "entering a pissing contest with a skunk," he grumbled to one colleague.[9]

"The headline 'Benchmark showing slight signs of strain in turbulent market' doesn't really make for a very good story, does it?" Ewan told a trade magazine in one interview from the period. "From our members, there is a perception that Libor remains about as accurate as you can get at the moment."[10]

Knight was equally recalcitrant when asked to comment on the issue by members of parliament at a hearing on financial stability in Westminster. "Libor has stood the test of two decades," she said, sounding mildly irritated. "Frankly, we have got a very sticky market out there; it is hardly surprising that you have rates that move in a different fashion than happened in the previous pretty benign conditions."[11]

When the Treasury committee's chairman pursued the line of questioning, she replied defiantly: "That does not mean that that is a problem with Libor. What that does is say this is what is happening in the market."

It was a disingenuous pitch. The truth was that both Knight and Ewan had every reason to suspect Libor was being nobbled. Every other day for months, Ewan had been contacted by some disgruntled banker or investor complaining that banks were quoting one rate and then borrowing in the market at a completely different one.[12] When a bank gave an obviously fictitious input, it was Ewan's job to call them up from his desk and set them straight. Harassed and overworked, he struggled to keep up, resorting on one occasion to slamming down his phone and crying: "You've got to be kidding me!" to the amusement of his colleagues.

The *Journal* article had merely served to draw the public's attention to a problem etched into Ewan's psyche. Liquidity, in financial-speak, refers to the ease with which one can access a market to buy or sell assets. For most of the century's first decade, banks had been swimming in it. Whenever a trader wanted to buy or sell a share, bond or derivative, he could count on somebody willing to take the other side of the trade. The same was true of cash. If a bank needed to borrow a couple of hundred million dollars for a few weeks, there would always be a lender somewhere happy to oblige in exchange for a small amount of interest.

By the summer of 2007, that had started to change. The mortgage crisis in the U.S. caused banks and investment funds around the world to become skittish about lending to each other without collateral. Firms that relied on the so-called money markets to fund their businesses were paralyzed by the ballooning cost of short-term credit. On Sept. 14, customers of Northern Rock queued for hours to withdraw their savings after the U.K. lender announced it was relying on loans from the Bank of England to stay afloat.

After that, banks were only prepared to make unsecured loans to each other for a few days at a time, and interest rates on longer-term loans rocketed. Libor, as a barometer of stress in the system, reacted accordingly. In August 2007, the spread between three-month dollar Libor and the overnight indexed swap, a measure of banks' overnight borrowing costs, jumped from 12 basis points to 73 basis points. By December it had soared to 106 basis points. A similar pattern could be seen in sterling, euros and most of the 12 other currencies published on the BBA's website each day at noon.

Everyone could see that Libor rates had shot up, but questions began to be asked about whether they had climbed enough to reflect the severity of the credit squeeze. By August 2007, there was almost no trading in cash for durations of longer than a month. In some of the smaller currencies there were no lenders for any time frame. Yet, with trillions of dollars tied to Libor, the banks had to keep the trains running. The individuals responsible for submitting Libor rates each day had no choice but to put their thumb and forefinger in the air and pluck out numbers. It was clear that their "best guesses" were unrealistically optimistic.

A game of brinkmanship had developed in which rate-setters tried to predict what their rivals would submit, and then come in slightly lower. If they guessed wrong and input rates higher than their peers, they would receive angry phone calls from their managers telling them to get back into the pack. On trading floors around the world, frantic conversations took place between traders and their brokers about expectations for Libor. Nobody knew where Libor should be, and nobody wanted to be an outlier. Even where bankers tried to be honest, there was no way of knowing if their estimates were accurate because there was no underlying interbank borrowing on which to compare them. The machine had broken down.

Now that the world's media had cottoned on to the problem, some-thing would need to be done. Knight's instinct was to try to pass respon-sibility for Libor to someone else. A Conservative member of parliament in the 1990s, she had seen her fair share of trouble. Weeks after her elec-tion in 1992, the Tories suffered a major blow when the U.K. was kicked out of the European Union's exchange-rate mechanism, which pegged sterling to the euro, an event known as Black Wednesday. In 1995, her appointment as Economic Secretary to the Treasury was overshadowed by the resignation of Prime Minister John Major; and her political career was cut short at the age of 46, when the opposition Labour Party blitzed the 1997 election with the biggest landslide in more than a century.

Knight recognized the potential problems with Libor early on. Since the days of Zombanakis, the rate had morphed from an esoteric bench-mark found in syndicated loan agreements to the basis for trillions of dollars of contracts, yet the resources devoted to overseeing it had not changed significantly. Libor may have represented a sizeable slice of rev-enue to the BBA, but, to Knight's mind at least, it was more trouble that it was worth. A few days after the first *Journal* article ran, she was invited to attend a meeting of senior government, regulatory and central bank offi-cials at the Bank of England's imposing 18th-century headquarters on Threadneedle Street. Knight asked whether it was appropriate to have such an important part of the global financial infrastructure in the hands of a relatively small London trade association.

Her question fell on deaf ears. Neither the Bank of England nor the Financial Services Authority had any desire to take on another source of problems during the worst financial crisis since the 1920s. The BBA would have to find its own solution. The trade group agreed to undertake a consultation, inviting anyone with any bright ideas on how to eradicate cheating and make Libor more accurate to write to them. Dozens of proposals arrived in the weeks that followed, from bankers, professors, lobbyists and senior public officials.

Among them was Tim Geithner, head of the New York Fed and one of the men leading the U.S. response to the crisis. Early in May, Gei-thner had attended a meeting of 50 or so central bankers in Basel, the Swiss city that's hosted similar get-togethers since the 1930s. Before the evening's customary dinner at the towering headquarters of the Bank for

International Settlements, Geithner met with Mervyn King, the governor of the Bank of England.

King, a railway porter's son who had made his name as an economics
professor at the University of Cambridge, was approaching the end of
a 20-year career at the U.K.'s central bank. At 61, he was more than
a decade older than the preppy Geithner, whose mother was a New
England aristocrat, but the two men shared a common purpose.

With the financial world ablaze, reforming Libor was considered in
some quarters a bit of a sideshow. But, as a measure of systemic stress,
its accuracy was crucial. At the end of April, King had announced the
U.K.'s "Special Liquidity Scheme (SLS)", through which banks could
swap the mortgage-backed securities clogging their balance sheets for
gilts until markets calmed down. Earlier that month the U.S. Federal
Reserve had lent banks $50 billion via its Term Auction Facility (TAF),
and it was gearing up to push out another $75 billion. Both the SLS and
the TAF were designed to hose liquidity back into the money markets
and encourage banks to start lending to each other and their customers
again.[13] The scorecard for the success of the measures was the impact
they had on short-term interest rates, as reflected by Libor. If Libor was
a fiction, who was to say that they were dealing with the problem at all?
Or that taxpayers' money was being targeted toward the right firms?

Geithner agreed to send King some suggestions for reforming the
benchmark, and on June 1, he e-mailed the governor and his deputy, Paul
Tucker, a list of recommendations prepared by his staff. They included
requiring banks to get their processes for setting Libor approved by external auditors, adding new banks to the Libor panels, culling some of the
more obscure maturities such as four months and seven months, and basing the published rate on a random selection of bank submissions rather
than using those of each bank on every panel. If those modest proposals had been adopted, many of the problems that followed might have
been prevented.

In the end, two of the most powerful men in the global economy weren't making the decisions. Libor's destiny rested in the hands of
15 unnamed, middle-ranking bankers and a former call-center worker
in London. Despite its pervasiveness, the benchmark resided in a kind
of regulatory wasteland. There were no references to it in any of the

myriad laws and regulations governing financial markets and no readily enforceable rules on how the rate should be set by individual traders or their employers.

Following the initial post-article bump in mid-April, Libor quickly slid back down to unrealistic levels. After several weeks of unwanted focus on their domain, the FXMMC gathered at Pinners Hall on May 19 to come up with a plan. There was something of a siege mentality in the meeting room.

"We need to adopt a minimal approach," said one banker, setting the tone early. "Too big a change would cause an explosive reaction."

Yes, one of his peers chimed. And we don't want to be coerced into anything "by outside sources such as the media".[14]

The banks on the committee had a sound reason to resist significant changes to the way Libor was set. By 2008, the benchmark was embedded in an estimated $350 trillion of derivatives contracts and $10 trillion of loans around the world.[15] To put that into perspective, the total amount of U.S. mortgage debt outstanding at the start of 2015 was $13 trillion. Any substantial alterations could have invalidated those contracts, some of which, in the case of interest-rate swaps, lasted decades.[16] On top of that, acknowledging serious flaws in Libor would have left the banks facing a barrage of litigation and legal wrangling.

The FXMMC concluded that the best option would be to change nothing and promise to do a better job of policing the rate. A lone banker pointed out that if they "change nothing, the media will raise questions about banks meeting and no outcome", but the decision had been made. Besides, they reassured each other, attention would die down once the crisis abated.

Over the following weeks, representatives from the Bank of England, the New York Fed, the BBA and the FSA butted heads in e-mails and on phone calls over what approach to adopt. Every time a serious reform was mooted, the banks resisted it. At one stage, King grew so frustrated with the proposals coming from the BBA that he hand-scrawled a note to Tucker that simply read: "This seems wholly inadequate. What should we do?"[17]

The answer, in the end, was nothing. King may have been unhappy with the attitude of the banks, but the Bank of England wasn't prepared to impose its will or take on responsibility for overseeing the rate. Forcing banks to make honest submissions at that point would have been deeply unhelpful to the central bank's efforts to prop up the banking system. It was a precarious time, and any bank that was merely perceived to have fallen behind was in danger of going bankrupt. It was a scab King and his colleagues understandably didn't want to pick.

The New York Fed also eventually walked away, unwilling or unable to force the issue on an obdurate British establishment. If it had ongoing concerns about the benchmark, that did not stop it from pegging $85 billion of loans to beleaguered insurer American International Group to Libor in September 2008, or $1 trillion to banks and investment firms via the Libor-linked Term Asset-Backed Securities Loan Facility two months later.

One group notable by its complete lack of engagement in the discussions was the FSA, the U.K. regulator ultimately responsible for overseeing the banks. Like the Bank of England, the FSA would later argue that Libor was unregulated and therefore fell through the cracks, but the body had the power to launch an investigation into allegations of improper behavior at any time. The decision not to do so was taken by senior staff including Thomas Huertas, an ex-banker from New York with a neatly clipped silver beard who had joined the FSA in 2004 and was now the director for banking supervision. Huertas had spent most of his career at Citigroup, one of the firms identified by the *Journal* as making dubious Libor submissions.

On May 29, 2008, the afternoon the second *Journal* story appeared, Huertas had ordered his team to undertake an analysis of the newspaper's methodology, which compared banks' Libor submissions with their credit default swap prices to suggest lowballing was rife. They came back with a list of minor errors with the paper's analysis, including that the reporters had compared three-month Libors with six-month CDS prices, and confused Citibank, a subsidiary, with Citigroup, the holding company. No matter that the broad thrust of the reporters' work turned out to be on the money. It was enough for Huertas to justify dropping the matter.

During the crisis, Huertas was one of the BBA's primary contacts at the FSA. When the CFTC first contacted the British regulator at the end of April 2008 and asked for its assistance in investigating allegations of lowballing, he wrote to colleagues: "It is not clear to me what juris-diction if any they would have in the matter." He signed off on a plan for them to "explain that we are in discussions with the BBA" and "we are not inviting them to participate". It would be two years before the FSA joined the CFTC in launching a formal investigation of Libor, although during that period the U.K. regulator did help its counterparts in Wash-ington procure documents from the banks.

As head of banking supervision, Huertas was one of a handful of senior figures who helped formulate the U.K.'s response to the financial crisis from an office at the Treasury. Libor was important, they reasoned, but there were many other things that needed to get done, and it wasn't a regulated or controlled market.

The FSA and the Bank of England did dig their heels in over one thorny issue: whether there should be any reference to them included in the consultation paper on Libor that the BBA was putting together. Alive to the importance of perceptions, Knight repeatedly insisted that the central bank and the regulator publicly support the BBA. Both refused, and when the document was published all mention of their involvement in the reform process contained in earlier drafts had been removed.

On June 10, a bright, sunny day in the British capital, the BBA published "Understanding the Construction and Operation of Libor—Strengthening for the Future", a carefully crafted treatise that suggested the furor surrounding the benchmark was the result of a series of mis-understandings by journalists rather than any wrongdoing by the banks. That afternoon Stephen Green, HSBC's chairman and an ordained cler-gyman, presented the paper on the opening day of the BBA's annual con-ference to some 350 bankers and finance professionals who had gathered among the marble columns and crystal chandeliers of the 19th-century Gibson Hall. It read:

> Since its inception in 1985, BBA Libor has enjoyed a reputation for accuracy. However, just as the credit crunch has led to stress in the markets, and the breakdown of longstanding correlations in the pricing of assets, as a barometer of these markets, it has also been stressed. This has led to discussion of some of the BBA Libor currency fixes—particularly the dollar fix—within the financial community. This proper discussion has overflowed into commentary

in the media, and the BBA believes that it needs to correct a number
of misunderstandings and misperceptions.

Commentators in the press, the BBA suggested, were blind to the
intricacies of financial markets and had jumped to conclusions. Com-
paring Libor with other barometers of market strength, as the *Journal* had done with credit default swaps, was misguided because of the
many differences among them. And lenders who complained they were
unable to borrow cash at the rates banks posted to Libor were being
unrealistic: As smaller, riskier institutions, their interest payments were
inevitably going to be higher than the panel banks. The idea that traders
could seek to manipulate the benchmark was discarded in two sentences:
"Submitted rates are trimmed to screen out high or low rates and then
the average calculated. The trimming process removes outlying data as
well as preventing any individual bank from attempting to influence
the rates."

The changes the BBA proposed were trivial. A new committee
would be set up to monitor submissions, but it would be made up of
the same vested interests of the banks, along with a handful of institutional investors and other financial insiders. New banks would be added
to the panels where possible, although the BBA pointed out—perhaps
unsurprisingly given recent events—that no firms had come forward to
request entry into the Libor club in recent months. Over the next two
years the BBA had to battle to persuade the existing banks to stay on
the panels.[18]

Nowhere in the 15-page document did the BBA specifically identify
or address the root cause of the problem as described by the *Journal* and
other financial commentators: that banks were lowballing their Libor
submissions to escape the stigma of being singled out as a credit risk.
Banks and other interested parties were invited to submit any proposals
to the BBA, but when the final document was released in the week before
Christmas 2008, it was virtually unchanged.

After reading the BBA's paper, Mollenkamp, the author of the *Journal's* Libor stories, called Knight. The reporter had a reputation for being
quick tempered and was furious that the BBA had tried to discredit his
work and sweep the issue under the carpet. It was one in a series of heated
conversations between the journalist and the group's CEO. Mollenkamp

once grew so exasperated with Knight he reportedly called the BBA a "bunch of motherfuckers". No matter. For now, at least, the bankers had succeeded in quelling the uprising. The Bank of England and the FSA may have kept their names out of the official documents, but behind the scenes they had stood by and allowed it to happen. Together, they opened the gate to the worst period of market manipulation in the history of financial markets.[19]

Chapter 8

The Sheep Will Follow

In Tokyo, Hayes was sent the April 2008 *Wall Street Journal* article by Sarah Ainsworth, his ex-girlfriend, but he brushed it off as irrelevant: Lowballing in dollar Libor had nothing to do with his yen derivatives book. It was just "headline grabbing journalism". Hayes told her. The prospect of a BBA review didn't much concern him either. Hayes dismissed the body that governed the rate as a toothless, ineffectual organization run by "a bunch of old blokes sat around a table drinking port".[1]

It wasn't that Hayes thought he was invincible. But with banks routinely underreporting their borrowing costs by as much as 40 basis points, the trader saw his efforts to tweak the rate by a quarter or half a basis point as small beer and not something regulators would bother investigating.[2] E-mails discovered by prosecutors suggest that Read, his broker at ICAP, had begged him to make his Libor requests more subtle, pointing out in one message that "compliance is a big thing in London now". Rather than e-mailing Goodman with Hayes's requests, Read had taken to texting his colleague from his iPhone. He'd even come up with a code word for Libor—"arbi"—to use in e-mails and messages. But Hayes seldom bothered. He thought Read was being paranoid.

Read would later say at trial that there were no compliance concerns—he was simply trying to scare Hayes into keeping the arrangement quiet in case his other clients got wind and felt the UBS trader was getting preferential treatment. He said the use of code words was for the same reason.

Hayes was making money, and his bosses were happy. That was all he really cared about. And by the time Lehman Brothers fell in September 2008, he believed his Libor scheme was working better than ever. With money markets, the cardiovascular system of the financial body, in arrest, rate-setters no longer had any idea what Libors to submit. Desperate for information, they phoned their brokers each morning and asked them what they were seeing in the market—brokers who were by now reliant on Hayes for the commissions that determined their annual bonuses. Adrift with no compass, many of the traders simply parroted the figures the brokers gave them without a second thought. Two banks—WestLB and Citigroup—didn't deviate from Goodman's predictions for weeks at a time. Read referred to them as the "sheep".[3] He would later state that he used the description to help convince Hayes he was successfully influencing the rate.

Life as a short-end interest-rate derivatives trader during the crisis was pretty good. Markets were highly volatile and that meant wider spreads, which, for market makers like Hayes, meant bigger profits. The difference in the cost of borrowing cash overnight compared with taking out a six-month loan had blown out to unprecedented levels. Whereas the spread between the two rates used to average about 7 basis points, and jumped around by less than 1 basis point day to day, it now stood at closer to 50 basis points. The flip side was that the risk of incurring losses was higher, but Hayes was routinely making more money in one day than he had in a week before the crisis.

His success had started to draw attention. In the summer of 2008, U.S. firm Goldman Sachs had approached Hayes about a job, offering him a $4.5 million signing package.[4] Hayes declined. Despite all his newfound braggadocio he worried that he wasn't good enough to join the world's most prestigious investment bank.[5] Ever the trader, he told his bosses he wanted to stay out of loyalty to the firm that had brought him to Tokyo and negotiated a huge bonus on the back of it.[6]

While people on other desks were struggling to survive, Hayes had come out of the whirlwind of the Lehman collapse in better shape than ever. His only issue now was how to pay the brokers enough to keep them loyal. He believed he had taken care of Read through the inflated fixed fee UBS paid ICAP, but RP Martin's Farr was compensated on a per-trade basis. On Sept. 18, with the market frozen and only a small window in which both Tokyo and London markets were open, Hayes was finding it difficult to source deals big enough to pay him. Sitting at his desk, strung out after one of the most stressful weeks in his life, Hayes came up with a novel idea. He picked up the phone and called Farr in London.

"If you've got any mates, mate, who will do you like a net trade, I can like basically give you like, fucking, I don't know, a trillion three-month Libor/Tibor and take back a trillion three-month Libor/Tibor," Hayes told him.[7] "Obviously you'll net it with the other guy."

Hayes was proposing a so-called wash trade, where counterparties place matching deals through a broker minutes apart that cancel one another out but still trigger fees for the middleman. The deal he was outlining served no commercial purpose and was purely a means to pay Farr large amounts of "bro"—slang for commission.

"If sixes go up a load, mate, I can't afford to do it," Hayes warned, referring to the six-month rate. "But if that happens, it's a 62,000 buck trade for you, alright."

It took some explaining before Farr fully understood what Hayes was proposing, but once he did, he was overjoyed. "All right, let's see what we can do," the broker said, laughing. "Fucking hell. All right."

Hayes claimed in court he was concerned enough about the probity of the wash trades to get up from his desk and seek approval from his boss, Mike Pieri, before going ahead, although there is no evidence he ever did. To Hayes's mind at least they were a good deal for the bank.[8] In one sense, they were stealing money from UBS to pay the brokers. But, Hayes reasoned, the economic value the bank received as a result of the trades far outweighed any brokerage paid on them.[9]

Unfortunately, not everyone shared his pragmatic point of view. The following day Hayes and Farr struggled to find anyone willing to take the other side of the transaction. Traders who had been happy to help out days earlier by tweaking their submissions balked at the idea of entering into a trade whose only purpose was to pay fees to one of Hayes's brokers. At some firms they were forbidden. Eventually Hayes persuaded JPMorgan's Stuart Wiley to agree to a relatively paltry 50 billion yen, or 260 million pounds, although there's no indication Wiley knew the deal was intended as a payment for the broker's help in moving Libor. Hayes still had 150 billion yen to go to pay Farr the £62,000 he'd been promised.[10]

After contacts at Merrill Lynch and Rabobank declined to participate, Farr turned to a colleague on his desk at RP Martin, Lee Aarons, for help. Aarons, known as Village in the market, said he knew just the man for the job. He called one of his best clients, Neil Danziger, a trader at RBS in London.

"Alright, geez, can you do me a favor? You're not going to pay any bro for this and we'll send you lunch around for the whole desk," Aarons said in the rapid-fire delivery unique to financial brokers. "Take it from UBS, give it back to UBS. He wants to pay some bro."

Putting business through favored brokers as a reward for directing trades your way or to acknowledge a particularly expensive meal the night before is standard practice across financial markets. The difference this time was there was no genuine trading going on—Hayes was effectively dealing with himself.

Privately educated at the exclusive West London boarding school St. Paul's, where poet John Milton and World War II hero Field Marshal Bernard Montgomery had been before him, Danziger had a penchant for the good life. He and Aarons had spent many hours—and thousands of pounds—working their way through London's best restaurants and hottest nightclubs on the broker's expense account. The two men were close, so when Aarons reached out, Danziger agreed to take the other side of the trade.

Later that day, Aarons promised to send lunch to the RBS trading floor for Danziger and his colleagues.

"Sri Thong," Danziger told him, referring to an expensive Thai restaurant nearby. "We'll pick it up. What's our limit? Last time we spent £500."

"I know mate, you fucking rascals," Aarons chuckled. "Hey listen thanks for doing that today, mate, it was fucking needed, it was like—we made a lot of money out of that."

It was ironic it was Aarons who had ridden to the rescue that day. When Hayes had started trading at RBS in 2002, he had been assigned Village, but the two never got on. After one particularly acute display of perceived incompetence, Hayes had shouted for Aarons to "just put the cleaner on the line" as they would do a better job.[11]

That afternoon, in a series of conversations after the wash trades had gone through, Hayes told Farr that this was how he was going to pay him in the future. "If you help me I'll help you," Hayes said. "It's a two-way street."

"We always fight your side, but yesterday we did make a fucking extra big effort mate," Farr said, milking the moment for all it was worth. "We really did. And we did sort of take the piss out of it a bit as well and it worked, so it's fucking good work."

Over the next 11 months, Hayes carried out 16 wash trades, generating more than £450,000 in kickbacks for his brokers.[12] Each time Farr bagged one he performed a little jig around his desk. There's no suggestion that Danziger, who was the counterparty on all of them bar one, knew that the trades were payments for help moving Libor. The quid pro quo for him was nights out at top-end nightclubs like Mahiki and trips to Las Vegas and Singapore.[13] In one year, Aarons claimed about £21,000—£400 a week—for entertaining Danziger, who was also being wined and dined by brokers at Tullett Prebon and ICAP.[14] Still, considering RP Martin earned £35,854 in brokerage fees on the first wash trade alone, it was good value for money.

Danziger was a market maker in some of the same yen interest-rate derivatives as Hayes, and, while the pair weren't close, their paths had crossed before. When the South African-born trader joined RBS from Standard Chartered in 2002, Hayes was a junior on the desk. Danziger left the U.K. to work in the New York office shortly after, but they bumped into each other from time to time. In the close-knit world of yen derivatives traders, everyone knew everyone else to some extent.

With short brown, wavy hair and a cheeky smile, Danziger had a reputation for playing as hard as he worked. Often he would go out with one of his brokers until the early hours, but no matter where the night took them, he always abided by the golden rule that a trader must be at his desk when the market opens. Convention dictates that brokers spend 3, 4 or even 5 percent of the revenue they earn from a trader on travel and entertainment. The more extravagant the expense, the more business the broker can expect to come his way. It became a running joke at UBS that Danziger only agreed to the wash trades because he was planning another trip.[15]

In the years before the financial crisis and the introduction of the Bribery Act in 2011, traders led a gilded existence. Tullett Prebon invited its customers to party in Las Vegas. ICAP took them skiing. Traders would think nothing of being chauffeured to horseraces at Ascot, flown by helicopter to Manchester for a football match or sent first class on the Eurostar for tennis at Roland Garros in Paris. While the venues and hosts changed from trip to trip, the faces were the same and the format for the nights seldom varied—a boozy dinner followed by carousing at nightclubs and bars before moving on to a strip joint or a brothel for the ones who were up for it.

In the City of London, a few venues were renowned as broker hotspots. Jamies Wine Bar near Liverpool Street was to Tullett Prebon what "Brasrock" was for ICAP. At lunchtimes and from 5 p.m. each weekday it was rammed full of Tullett brokers and their clients. Older brokers—the "old school" as they were known—congregated in Dirty Dicks, a less salubrious pub. A Thai massage parlor above a nearby noodle shop did a roaring trade.

With half a dozen clients to entertain, some brokers found it hard to keep up the pace. Many were burned out by the time they were 40, succumbing to diabetes, depression, drug addiction or alcoholism. In January 2014, an RP Martin broker named Robin Clark was shot in the leg by a masked gunman near his home in Essex, earning the sobriquet "the Wolf of Shenfield". The day he returned to work, a couple of colleagues crept up behind him wearing balaclavas and screamed "Bang!" Clark fell off his chair, reopened the wound and was hospitalized.[16] At another of the firms Hayes used, two new potential recruits were pitted against each other on a night out in a bizarre initiation test. After being plied with alcohol and cocaine, the trainees were taken on a tour of strip clubs before ending the evening in a brothel. One passed out. The other stayed the distance and got the job.

One year, ICAP took half a dozen yen derivatives traders from banks including JPMorgan, RBS and Goldman Sachs to St. Anton, a ski resort in Austria. The trip was hosted by Read's boss on the medium-term yen interest-rate swaps desk in London, Danny Wilkinson. Short and bull-necked, with a distinct swagger and the patter of a trader at a market stall, Wilkinson was a legendary bon vivant with a passion for collecting fine wine and the ruddy complexion to match. A former trader himself, he peppered his speech with cockney slang like "bish bash bosh" and "aye aye shepherd's pie", a wink to the notorious Hayes anecdote from a few years before. Like Read and Goodman, he had joined Godsell in the 1980s. Since then he'd risen through the ranks to a director role and, in a good year, a seven-figure package.

It was Wilkinson who helped arrange the £15,000 a quarter "Libor services fee" UBS paid ICAP to skew its daily run-through to suit Hayes's book, according to ICAPs $87 million settlement with the FCA and the CFTC. Wilkinson, who was acquitted of being part of a conspiracy in a London court in 2016, said the payment was simply for the information ICAP provided. No other banks paid ICAP a "Libor services fee".

On the ski trip, Paul Glands, a senior JPMorgan trader who'd just become a father, was the butt of many of the jokes because his wife made him wear a helmet on the slopes. After one particularly heavy night that culminated in a play fight, Glands wound up in the hospital with a head injury. That only made the mocking worse because Glands was the only one on the trip who couldn't claim to have injured himself skiing.

While most traders were happy accepting the brokers' largesse, Hayes was a different beast: He got drunk on a couple of pints, didn't enjoy social events and preferred KFC to fine dining. Hayes disdained the hedonistic culture prevalent among Tokyo's expat bankers. He didn't understand how someone could blow $20,000 or $30,000 on a night out.[17] Hayes would rather go home early, have an orange juice and be fresh the following morning to do what he loved most—trade.

Still, he was not beyond the occasional indulgence. When Hayes whisked Tighe away on a romantic holiday to Thailand in April 2009, RP Martin picked up the $5,000 hotel tab.[18] Then there were the £1,000 candle-lit meals at Michelin-starred restaurants he'd bill Farr or Read for, and the cricket tickets Tullett Prebon obtained for Hayes's family to watch England do battle against the Australians. ICAP was so desperate to keep him happy, they bent their own rules on client entertainment, paying £1,500 a ticket for him to see Floyd Mayweather fight Ricky Hatton in Las Vegas in 2007. "Whilst I do not usually sanction buying expensive tickets for customers, in the unusual case that is Tom,

I feel it is worth it," ICAP's managing director David Casterton, known as "Clumpy", wrote to a fellow executive at the time.[19]

For Hayes, the wash trades weren't repayment for expensive nights out. They were about consolidating his control over the brokers. When they pleased him, he rewarded them. When they didn't, he gave them hell. If Farr deigned to go on holiday during the busy month-end, Hayes berated him. The monthly payments of £30,000 or so were a drop in the ocean for Hayes, who took billion-dollar positions on a daily basis. But for brokers like Farr, who got a sizeable percentage, they were the difference between hitting their monthly targets and coming up short. The wash trades alone accounted for nearly 9 percent of the revenue on Farr's desk in 2008, on top of all the additional legitimate business Hayes threw his way. Farr depended on Hayes, who worked him like a marionette. Whatever it cost, it was worth it. Hayes brought in $80 million in 2008, almost double the previous year.[20] Hayes never thought to question the loyalty of his lieutenants. In his eyes, there seemed to be no limit to what he could achieve.

Chapter 9

Escape to London

G ary Gensler's swearing-in ceremony at the CFTC on May 26, 2009, was carefully orchestrated for maximum impact, as with most events in his life. In a speech at the agency's headquarters just after 4:30 p.m., Gensler thanked President Obama before paying his dues to the people who had helped him get there: Pete Rouse and Jim Messina, Obama's future chief of staff and campaign manager; former Treasury Secretary Larry Summers, Gensler's old mentor and now an economic adviser to the White House; Phil Schiliro, the president's director of legislative affairs.

Senior CFTC staffers jostled for seats with journalists and Washington movers and shakers, including Treasury Secretary Geithner and the recently appointed chairman of the Securities and Exchange Commission (SEC), Mary Schapiro. On a wall hung a defibrillator machine, a fitting visual metaphor for Gensler's mission to revive a government agency that lacked credibility and firepower.

"Our financial and regulatory systems have failed the American people," Gensler said, elongating his vowels. "As chairman of the CFTC, I will work vigorously to use every tool and authority available to us to protect the American people from fraud, manipulation and excessive speculation."

Gensler describes himself to friends as "a short, bald Jew from Baltimore". At 5-foot-7 and no more than 150 pounds he may be physically unimposing, but his razor-sharp intellect and forthright personality allow him to dominate any room he finds himself in.

Gensler's appointment marked a step up for the CFTC. A former high-ranking executive at Goldman Sachs, he turned his back on Wall Street at the age of 39 having amassed a reported fortune of about $60 million, making him Obama's richest appointee.[1] Between 1997 and 2001, Gensler served as a Treasury official in the Clinton administration, and in 2002 he was one of the architects of the Sarbanes-Oxley Act, which overhauled accounting standards and bolstered corporate governance after the Enron and WorldCom scandals.

A father of three daughters, Gensler took a career break in the years surrounding his wife Francesca's death from breast cancer in June 2006, before returning as an adviser to Hillary Clinton during her bid for the Democratic nomination in 2008. Less than a week after Clinton dropped out of the race he offered his services to the Obama camp. He used his connections to drum up support among CEOs and was rewarded with a place on the transition team for the SEC.

Gensler made sure he expressed how proud and thankful he was to be given the CFTC job in his speech on that Tuesday afternoon, but privately he admitted to friends he felt a degree of disappointment. Newspaper articles had linked him to the more prestigious SEC chairmanship, and as head of the transition team he was the obvious candidate. Instead, he had lost out to Schapiro, who had more experience probing Wall Street's excesses. In his first stint in government, Gensler had served Robert Rubin in the Treasury alongside Geithner, but it was Geithner who now occupied Rubin's old seat at the heart of government.

Still, Gensler's appointment coincided with a marked increase in the CFTC's powers. Two weeks earlier, Geithner had published a letter outlining sweeping reforms to the $700 trillion swaps market. It was a response to the devastating role derivatives had played in causing the financial crisis. Under the new rules, which Gensler helped formulate, some swaps would be traded on public exchanges in the same way as stocks, and the companies that traded them would be forced to put up collateral to independent clearing houses. Responsibility for drafting the rules and the ongoing oversight of the market would fall to the CFTC. Although he didn't know it at the time, Gensler also inherited the CFTC during the early stages of what would become one of the biggest investigations into financial malfeasance ever undertaken by a government agency: Libor.

Not everyone backed him to do a good job. Of the 30 presidential appointees put before the Senate that year, Gensler was the last to be approved. His selection as head of the CFTC was blocked for months by Democrat Maria Cantwell and independent Bernie Sanders, who questioned whether he was the right person to help "create a new culture in the financial marketplace" after the crisis.

It wasn't just Gensler's background in banking that provoked skepticism. As an undersecretary to Rubin, Gensler had played a prominent role in pushing through the Commodity Futures Modernization Act of 2000, which exempted over-the-counter derivatives such as interest-rate swaps and credit default swaps from regulation. At the time, the head of the CFTC, Brooksley Born, had warned the government it was making a mistake, but she was roundly ignored by heavyweights including Fed Chairman Alan Greenspan.

That decision ushered in the explosive growth of derivatives, which turbocharged the global financial meltdown. In the end, Gensler went before the Senate and issued a *mea culpa*, admitting that Born had been right and promising to help bring in a new era of strict oversight of the banks.

Gensler, a natural pragmatist, didn't see the volte-face as some kind of Damascene conversion. When he was a banker, his goal was to make money, and he embraced it wholeheartedly. Now that he was a regulator, his job was to curb the banks and make the system safer, and he was going to attack it with the same vim and determination. Whatever he was doing he wanted to be the best and, almost as importantly according to friends, be acknowledged as such. Gensler didn't change. Only the role did.

Gensler was born on Oct. 18, 1957, three minutes before his identical twin Robert. His father ran a business supplying cigarette machines and penny arcades to Baltimore bars. His mother also worked for the company, on top of looking after the five children. Neither of their parents had been to college, yet Gary and his brother thrived. Their ability with numbers was clear at an early age. As teenagers they were sent to a summer camp for mathematically precocious youth at Johns Hopkins University.

At 17, they arrived at the Wharton School of the University of Pennsylvania, where they competed for top billing. In one freshman economics class, the professor announced there were just two students who had scored higher than 50 points on an exam. Robert passed a note to his brother letting him know he was one of them, with 51, to which Gary sent one back saying: "We must be twins: 51."[2]

That sense of competition would continue throughout their careers. In 2002, Gary co-authored *The Great Mutual Fund Trap*, a 350-page denunciation of the fund management industry. By then Robert was a highly regarded fund manager at T. Rowe Price Group in Baltimore, and the twins appeared on talk shows as a double-act, arguing out their positions.

After completing his MBA at Wharton in 1979, Gensler was hired at age 21 by Goldman Sachs. It was there he honed his skills for bluff and negotiation, working on big-ticket media deals like the National Football League's $3.6 billion television rights sale. Every two years Goldman anoints a new crop of partners to share in its vast profits, and at 30 Gensler was invited to join the club. At the time he was the second-youngest partner in the firm's 110-year history, behind only private equity magnate Chris Flowers, who joined the same week as Gensler but was born a few days after him.

At Goldman, Gensler was surrounded by future titans of business and politics. In 1983, he spent a year on rotation with the bank's risk-arbitrage desk, which bet large sums on whether or not announced M&A deals would complete. His colleagues included Tom Steyer, who would go on to start Farallon Capital Management; Eddie Lampert, who founded ESL Investments; and Richard Perry, the founder of Perry Capital. The three hedge-fund managers are now worth a combined $5 billion, according to *Forbes* magazine, leading Gensler to quip: "Maybe I should have stayed there." Other alumni include Treasury Secretary Hank Paulson.

A few years after making partner, Gensler was dispatched to Tokyo to run the fixed-income, currencies and commodities trading business. By then he was married to an Italian-American artist with an MBA from Columbia, Francesca Danieli, and the couple had two daughters under three years old. They lived in Roppongi, the same well-to-do neighborhood Tom Hayes would move to. About a third of the $300 million in revenue Gensler oversaw came from trading yen-based swaps, the very instruments Hayes and his counterparts bought and sold.

"I helped manage and oversee a lot of yen Libor swaps, but I didn't explore then: 'Should we trust yen Libor?' Gensler recalls over milkshakes at the American City Diner near his home in Chevy Chase, an upscale Washington neighborhood. "Frankly, in the '80s and '90s at Goldman Sachs I was just as accepting intellectually about Libor as everybody else."

In 1994, he returned with his family to New York to co-run Goldman's finance function, a complex balancing act that involved shipping money between the bank's 700 or so legal entities to minimize taxes and fund a multibillion dollar balance sheet. There he discovered how pervasive Libor was. Every trading desk around the world had its own profit-and-loss account whose inventory was calculated with reference to Libor. Desks within the bank were funded internally at Libor plus a spread depending on how risky they were.

"Now that I have the benefit of hindsight I can look back and say, 'Why didn't I personally question it?'" Gensler says. "But we took for granted it was an independent rate."

The first two months of Gensler's tenure at the CFTC were spent preparing the agency for the herculean task of getting the swaps rules through Congress. It was not until a short meeting with members of the enforcement division in July 2009 that he learned about the nascent investigation into Libor. As the division's directors shuffled out of Gensler's ninth-floor office, down a hallway lined with the portraits of past chairmen, he called back acting head Steve Obie.

"Steve, I was reading something about problems with Libor. You think there might be something there?" Gensler asked, motioning for Obie to sit down on a sofa in a small alcove in a corner of the room. It was one of their first private meetings. The *Financial Times* had just published an article questioning why Libor rates remained so low when issuance of commercial paper, a form of short-term loan between banks, had fallen off a cliff. If banks weren't lending to each other, the benchmark should have risen sharply.[3]

"Well, the good news is we're already looking at it," replied Obie.

Obie explained how, spurred by *The Wall Street Journal*'s articles the previous year, the division had begun gathering intelligence and making contact with some of the banks that contributed to the rate.

"Great; if this is true, it could be huge," Gensler said. He had already recognized that if the CFTC was going to be taken seriously, it would need to switch its focus from small-time Ponzi schemers to Wall Street. "Get me a briefing together."

Obie caught an elevator down to the seventh floor and sighed. What he declined to share with Gensler was that the Libor investigation had hit a brick wall. Shortly after McGonagle, Lowe and Termine had sat down in April 2008 to map out a strategy for investigating the benchmark, events conspired to undermine their efforts. In July of that year, then-chairman Walt Lukken announced he had selected Obie to succeed Greg Mocek as acting head of enforcement instead of the more senior McGonagle. At the time, Obie was running the CFTC's enforcement division in New York, but now he would be based in Washington in a large office near McGonagle, his former boss. Inevitably the rivalry between the two men flared.

That summer McGonagle's father had a stroke, leaving him needing round-the-clock care. Around the same time Termine, the hard-talking attorney assigned by McGonagle to run the investigation day to day, became pregnant. By the end of the year she was on maternity leave with a child she would later jokingly refer to as "the Libor baby" because of the timing.

Meanwhile, the agency was up to its neck in crude oil. Since the onset of the financial crisis oil prices had skyrocketed by 40 percent, and the rise was being blamed in some quarters on unfettered speculation in commodity futures. The CFTC was under pressure to do something. On May 29, 2008, it announced it was stepping up its surveillance of the market to root out any manipulation. The frenzy died down eventually, but for the next year, about half of the enforcement division's 100 employees were assigned to the case.

With so much focus on oil, the embryonic Libor investigation had ground to a halt. The truth was that many of the banks they'd written to in April 2008 had been ignoring them anyway. While the CFTC had jurisdiction over global derivatives and futures markets, it did not directly oversee the banks themselves, and they were understandably reluctant to offer up information unless they had to.

Adopting a "memorandum of understanding" that allows for the sharing of documents between the 120 members of the International

Organization of Securities Commissions, the CFTC asked the FSA to jimmy the banks in London along. The FSA agreed on the condition that it could review anything that passed through its hands. Still, by the summer of 2009 nothing significant had come into either agency from any of the banks.

Meanwhile, after initially agreeing to assist the CFTC with its inquiries, the BBA had undergone a change of heart. In February 2009, six months after the CFTC first requested information, the lobbying group wrote to the agency suggesting that its investigation into Libor manipulation was misguided and stating that it was seeking legal advice about whether it was required to forward any documents. It is little wonder the banks did not feel obliged to cooperate with the CFTC: The BBA's letter was endorsed on Jan. 30 by the FSA's own director of banking supervision, former Citigroup banker Thomas Huertas.[4]

In the weeks that followed, Obie did his best to avoid Gensler in the corridors of the CFTC, and on Sunday, Oct. 4, 2009, he escaped the city altogether to catch a flight to London. He was a speaker on a panel at Commodities Week, a three-day event for traders, bankers and lawyers from around the world. In the muffled beige and maroon of the Royal Garden Hotel overlooking Hyde Park, Obie explained how the CFTC's powers were set to increase under the incoming regulations.

Also on the panel that day was Mocek, Obie's predecessor as head of enforcement at the CFTC. Mocek had left in September 2008, a week before Lehman Brothers collapsed, to become a partner at McDermott Will & Emery, a 1,100-attorney firm headquartered in Chicago. With his bald pate, spectacles and impeccable manners, Mocek projected the air of a Southern gentleman. Whenever possible he liked to head back to his native Louisiana to shoot ducks.

Mocek's rapid ascent through the ranks at the CFTC had surprised and frustrated some of his colleagues. A life-long Republican, he'd catapulted from trial attorney to head of enforcement before his fortieth birthday, bypassing layers of middle management. Still, even his detractors couldn't refute his success. Enforcement actions rose during his tenure, and it was on his watch that the agency fined more than two dozen of the country's largest energy firms for manipulating natural gas prices.

Over the years, Obie and Mocek had become friends, and when Mocek had a serious car accident, Obie visited him in hospital. After the London panel discussion the two men met up in the lounge of the Grosvenor House hotel for a drink.

"So, I've been looking into Libor for Barclays," Mocek said, leaning in. "You're not going to believe what we've found."

Shortly after Mocek had joined McDermott, the firm had been appointed by Barclays to advise it on the CFTC's Libor inquiry. It's common for companies facing legal problems to hire former enforcement officials in the hope they can influence their case, and with the government's post-crisis clampdown on derivatives, ex-CFTC personnel were suddenly in high demand.

Mocek explained that, after carrying out a preliminary internal investigation into Libor, Barclays staff had unearthed e-mails, phone recordings and instant messages that seemed to corroborate the CFTC's suspicions: Libor was routinely being gamed by the banks that set it.

Obie was transfixed. And that isn't all, Mocek continued. Some of the conversations the bank had found involved derivatives traders in New York putting pressure on their colleagues in London to change their submissions to suit their trading positions.

It was a bombshell. Until then, the CFTC had been entirely focusing on whether banks were suppressing Libor during the crisis to give the impression they were healthier than they were. As far as the authorities were concerned, this was a whole new category of malfeasance.

"You guys better be ready," Mocek said, draining his drink. "Libor is being manipulated, and it's going to be huge." Obie stayed behind for a few moments, shell-shocked. The following day he packed his bags and caught a flight back to Washington to tell his colleagues they had a case on their hands.

Chapter 10

Goodbye, Big Nose

After single-handedly saving UBS tens of millions of dollars following the collapse of Lehman Brothers, Hayes saw out the year in style with a trip to Las Vegas with Sarah Tighe. The couple had been together just over a year, and Hayes had never been happier. What he'd done to deserve this intelligent, attractive woman he didn't know, but he was smitten. As the clock counted down to midnight on New Year's Eve, amid the bright lights of the Strip, Hayes asked Tighe to marry him. She said yes.

Confident, mature and outgoing, Tighe was in many ways the opposite of her fiancé. Where Hayes had to be reminded to change his clothes in the morning, Tighe dressed sharply in knee-length dresses or skirts, short tailored jackets and high heels. Before they went to social events, Tighe, who had studied psychology at university, would tell Hayes not to ask people how much they earned or comment on their weight.[1] Sometimes it seemed she was more like his mother than his partner. But Hayes was brilliant, passionate about what he did and, when he wanted to be, quite charming. He was like no one she'd ever met and she was fiercely protective of him.

While things were going well in his personal life, professionally, 2009 couldn't have gotten off to a worse start. In December, Read, his closest confidante, had retired from the market. For years the ICAP broker had set his alarm for 2:30 a.m. and made his way to a desolate trading floor to cover the Asian markets from London. He had hoped for a change of pace when he moved to New Zealand the previous year, but he wound up working just as hard to keep his only client happy, rarely getting home before 10 p.m. So he handed in his notice and moved with his family to the coast of New Zealand's South Island. Read was looking forward to exploring the beaches of the Bay of Plenty and learning to surf before maybe retraining as a geography teacher.[2] Hayes was bereft. Not only was Read an excellent broker and source of information, he was also the closest thing Hayes had to a friend in the market. If Hayes was having family problems or struggling at work, it was Read he confided in.

"Words cannot adequately express how much I have enjoyed working with you," Hayes wrote to Read in a long farewell e-mail. "This year has been the pinnacle of my career and you played a huge part in it. In short, you are irreplaceable and I am gutted that you are going. I am eternally grateful for the support you gave me during the difficult times and apologize for all the times I have been less than civil or outright rude, you managed to cope with my moods really well."

Hayes continued using ICAP's services in London, but no one came close to matching the dedication he received from Read, and he threatened to pull his business several times. Read's former colleagues in London thought Hayes, whose commissions were now being divvied up between them and ICAP's Tokyo office, was a bully and a nuisance. They had their own roster of clients to look after and took to ignoring his phone calls. With Read gone, Hayes's link to Goodman and his run-through e-mail had also weakened. He still made requests to Wilkinson, who promised to help, but he was never sure whether the yen derivatives desk head passed them on or was just paying lip service.

Without Read and his sway over Lord Libor's run-through, Hayes worried he was in danger of losing his edge. He would need to find a new recruit if he was to continue exerting any control over the benchmark. He turned his attention to Tullett Prebon, the second-biggest interdealer brokerage firm after ICAP.

Noel Cryan was among the first brokers Hayes had met as a wet-behind-the-ears trainee at RBS in London. Cryan had left school in Lewisham, South East London, at 17 and found his way into the industry after spells as a bookmaker and a laborer. Now in his forties, he had grown pasty from spending so many hours in the glare of his computer.

A lifelong supporter of the notoriously rough East London soccer team Millwall—who chant "no one likes us, we don't care" at matches—Cryan and Hayes bonded over their love of football.

At Tullett, Cryan managed a small team of derivatives brokers. Hayes placed a fair amount of business through him, but since Cryan had no contact with the Libor-setters he hadn't asked him for help moving the benchmark. Until now. The moment Cryan logged on to his Bloomberg at 7 a.m. on Feb. 9, 2009, Hayes fired off a message. "Do you know your cash desk?" Hayes wrote. "Ie the guy who covers yen on your cash desk."

Tullett's cash desk—the brokers who interacted with the rate-setters and stood the best chance of influencing their submissions—was situated on the other side of a row of lockers from Cryan's spot in the middle of the firm's London trading floor. Hayes had always considered them third rate, but he was desperate.

Hayes outlined the system he had in place with RP Martin and ICAP: How, in return for payments, the cash brokers agreed to help him move Libor by asking rate-setting banks for favors or lying to them about which direction they expected the benchmark to move. If Cryan got his cash desk to do the same, Hayes promised, it would "come back to you in spades".

Cryan agreed immediately. Rumors of RP Martin's arrangement with Hayes had been percolating in London's highly competitive broking community for a while. RP Martin was a minnow in interest rate derivatives, yet the firm was earning millions of pounds in brokerage fees from Hayes. A few months earlier, Cryan's boss, Angus Wink, had told him to try to poach Farr, Cryan later testified. Farr had come in for an interview, but in the end he'd decided to stay with RP Martin.

Shortly after Hayes made his pitch to Cryan, RBS trader Danziger was looking for a way to pay Tullett some brokerage as a down payment for his trip to Las Vegas. Hayes stepped in and agreed to take the other side of a wash trade. Within a week of contacting Cryan, Hayes had generated £52,819 in fees for the Tullett broker. It was a compelling attempt to buy his loyalty.

Hayes needed all the help he could get. It was becoming increasingly difficult for him to influence his own bank's Libor submissions. Hayes was a great trader but a nightmare of a colleague. He had few friends and, with his hair-trigger temper, made enemies easily. His personal hygiene was sometimes poor, which wasn't helped by his habit of wearing the same clothes when he was on a winning streak. One day, after he had gone home, his colleagues left some shower gel on his desk as a joke. When Hayes was promoted to executive director in October 2008, his bosses warned him that his conduct was unacceptable. His tendency to fly off the handle at the slightest provocation had left sales staff frightened to talk to him.

No one felt the full force of Hayes's mercurial nature more than Roger Darin, the manager in charge of UBS's yen rate-setters. Their relationship had deteriorated to such an extent that they barely spoke. Darin thought Hayes was a disrespectful, arrogant bully and hated that he treated him as if he were his junior. He complained to his bosses that Hayes was asking him to input rates that were so wildly inaccurate they risked undermining the credibility of the bank.[3] Though he was sometimes ordered to comply with the star trader's requests, he frequently refused and even input rates designed to hurt Hayes's positions out of spite. After one particularly ferocious row, the pair had to be physically separated.

For months, Hayes had been trying to bypass Darin by going straight to the low-ranking rate-setters in Zurich, Rolf Keiser and Joachim Ruh. E-mails unearthed by prosecutors appear to show that they agreed to nudge the rate. If that didn't work, he would ask his junior, Mirhat Alykulov, a genial young trader from Kazakhstan whom Hayes had been training, to ask for favors on his behalf. The Swiss Libor-setters were perfectly civil and helped out where they could, but ultimately their loyalty lay with their boss. A few months earlier Darin had been moved to the seat next to Hayes, and he spent hours chatting in Swiss German to the Zurich cash desk via video link, stoking Hayes's paranoia.

The civil war between Hayes and Darin was symptomatic of a wider schism between UBS's investment banking business, which incorporated rates trading, and the treasury and cash side of the bank, which had primary responsibility for safeguarding the firm's financial health. Since the onset of the crisis in 2007, the two sides had fundamentally different priorities and clashed constantly. Traders like Hayes saw the mayhem as a great opportunity to make as much money as possible and wanted the freedom to place ever-larger wagers, while those in group treasury were trying to de-risk the bank as they struggled to keep it afloat.

Eighteen months earlier, when investors started scrutinizing banks' Libor submissions as a gauge of their financial health, treasury had ordered the rate-setters to lowball their submissions.[4] In such sensitive markets they didn't want to be perceived as having credit problems. With the survival of the firm at stake, the needs of the derivatives traders were of secondary importance. Pieri, Hayes's boss, complained to senior management that his traders were effectively fighting with one hand tied behind their backs, but he was overruled.[5]

That was hardly surprising. UBS only narrowly avoided following Lehman Brothers into bankruptcy thanks to a $59 billion bailout from the Swiss government in October 2008. The firm posted a $17 billion loss that year, the biggest ever for a Swiss company.

By the spring of 2009, it was becoming increasingly obvious to Hayes that the bean counters were in the ascendency, and he started worrying for the first time about his future at UBS. The bank was being restructured, and Darin's yen short-term interest-rate trading team was being merged with Hayes's derivatives-trading division. The Zurich-based head of the cash business, Yvan Ducrot, a close ally of Darin's who shared his disdain for Hayes and his methods, had been promoted to head the new business globally. The first thing Ducrot told Hayes when they spoke by video link, Hayes would later testify, was that UBS wouldn't be honoring the $2.5 million bonus he'd been promised after he turned down Goldman Sachs's job offer. Hayes, who didn't have the bank's internal video-messaging system set up on his computer, was in Pieri's office. When Ducrot informed him he would only be getting $250,000 after the bank racked up huge losses, Hayes was livid and made his feelings clear. He reckoned he should be getting at least 5 percent of the $80 million he earned for the company the previous year. Instead he was getting less than 1 percent. Any sense of loyalty he felt to the firm was fast draining away.

When a headhunter called him one day in June and suggested a meeting with a Citigroup executive, Hayes jumped at the opportunity. The U.S. bank was a major player in bonds, stocks and currency trading but was relatively weak in rates, which had recently been among the biggest earners for Wall Street. Citigroup was looking to correct that and had hired dozens of former Lehman Brothers traders to build a new business. The push in Asia was being led by Chris Cecere, a small, goateed

American with a big reputation and an unerring eye for finding new ways to make money. At Lehman he'd set up a string of highly lucrative business lines and trading desks. Now he was hoping to do the same thing at Citigroup.

Hayes met Cecere, who'd studied biochemistry before entering finance, at the elegant, low-lit jazz bar at the Grand Hyatt Tokyo in Roppongi, a favorite with expat bankers, Hayes would later recall. Cecere had beer. Hayes stuck to orange juice and listened as the somewhat-dorky Cecere outlined plans to build a world-beating derivatives business with Hayes at the center. The rapport was immediate. Here was someone with vision at a bank with real ambition rather than one that was intent on clipping his wings.

When he told Pieri about the approach, Hayes's boss panicked and started lobbying UBS management to keep him. For all his prickly character traits, Hayes was still an incredible earner. By June 2009 he was up about $150 million for the year. Pieri e-mailed Ducrot and senior managers including Carsten Kengeter, the co-CEO of the investment bank, extolling Hayes's virtues as an "exceptional" trader with "excellent" risk-management skills. He even alluded to Hayes's methods, highlighting the trader's "strong connections with Libor setters in London" and how the information he gleaned from them was "invaluable for the derivatives book".

Pieri had always had Hayes's back. No matter how many rows Hayes started or salespeople he upset or phones he smashed, Pieri stood by him. It helped that Hayes made the desk a lot of money, but their connection ran deeper. Like Hayes, Pieri was devoted to his job, seldom leaving the office to socialize. Hayes was a few years younger than Pieri and looked to him for approval, describing him to his brokers as "the perfect boss".[6]

Ducrot forwarded Pieri's e-mail to Darin asking him for "some balancing points against this bullshit". From his e-mails, Darin seems only too happy to help.

"I find it embarrassing when he calls up his mates to ask for favors on high/low fixings," Darin replied in a long missive rebutting Pieri point by point. "It makes UBS appear to manipulate others to suit their positions. What's the legal risk of UBS asking others to move their fixing?"

The revelation that one of their top traders was trying to rig Libor doesn't appear to have rung any alarm bells with UBS's senior managers, who seemed more interested in Hayes's trading prowess. Hayes was promised another multimillion dollar bonus and received a series of fawning calls from executives. Hayes still felt some loyalty to UBS, and to Pieri in particular, but when he asked his bosses to put their promises in writing, they refused.

By now Hayes's fiancée had had enough of UBS's broken promises. As a lawyer, Tighe recognized the value of the written agreement, and when none was forthcoming she told Hayes to jump ship. She may have looked like a school prefect, but Tighe was a fighter and she wasn't going to let her future husband be taken advantage of. When Cecere lined up meetings for Hayes with some of Citigroup's biggest hitters, she pushed him to go.

One evening, the head of Citigroup's investment bank in Japan, Brian McCappin, a fellow Brit, called Hayes and asked him out for a drink. McCappin, who had toyed with pursuing a career as a rock musician in his youth, took Hayes to a karaoke bar and serenaded him. It was his favorite party trick, and Hayes lapped up the attention. At another meeting with Cecere, Hayes brought along his wife, who ended up doing most of the talking on his behalf.[7]

Hayes may have had one foot out the door, but he remained just as committed at work. While some people might have slacked off, arriving late and taking long lunches, Hayes's focus on his P&L never wavered. That June he began laying the groundwork for what would turn out to be his most audacious campaign yet.

Hayes had positioned his derivatives book to profit from an expected spike in six-month Libor in the days just before and after the end of June, reflecting a phenomenon known as the "turn". Borrowing rates historically tend to rise in the days around the end of each quarter as banks hoard cash in an attempt to window-dress their financial results. It was a quirk of the market that some traders didn't factor into their models early enough. Hayes thought of it as easy money and had $2 million riding on every basis point.

But by June 26, his plan was going awry. Central banks were flooding the system with cheap money, and Hayes was swimming against a tsunami of cash that was dragging Libor lower in all currencies. The yen rate had fallen more than 2 basis points in the past four days, and Hayes was drowning.

That afternoon, he set about trying to reverse his fortunes on a mobile phone call with Guillaume Adolph, a Deutsche Bank trader who also set his bank's Libors. Hayes knew Adolph, whom he called Gollum, from his time in London when the chain-smoking Frenchman was at Merrill Lynch. While they had scarcely met in person, they communicated regularly on instant messages and e-mails. Short, bald and thickset with an intense stare and fingernails bitten to the quick, Adolph was a kindred spirit. Both were whip smart, lived to trade and weren't afraid to bet the bank. It was that tendency that had led to Adolph's abrupt departure from Merrill Lynch. He was one of a handful of traders Hayes respected, and they often swapped ideas. E-mails suggest that for the past 10 months the pair had also been periodically coordinating their Libor submissions.

Hayes proposed a deal, but before the details could be ironed out, the batteries on his aging Nokia ran out. Hayes had struggled to understand Adolph's thick accent so, in a move that would come back to haunt him years later, he bashed out an instant message reiterating what he understood their agreement to be: If Adolph increased his six-month yen submission in the coming days, Hayes would mobilize his network to help him out with whatever he needed.[8]

"For the next 2 weeks I really really need you to put 6m higfher," Hayes wrote.

"What is teh adte just that I know?" Adolph responded.

"July 14," Hayes said. "After that I need 6m to crash off…Like you."

"That is no problem for me," Adolph replied.

Until now, Hayes's efforts to skew the benchmark had been focused on the next few days. This was different. What he had agreed with Adolph involved dictating where Libor would fix weeks into the future, when it was impossible to know where any bank would be able to borrow.

Adolph increased his six-month Libor inputs a staggering 16 basis points over the next two days. His intervention helped push the published rate almost 1 basis point higher on June 29, saving Hayes close to $2 million. Adolph was sacked from Deutsche Bank in 2011 but never charged. He denies any wrongdoing, claiming he only ever fobbed Hayes off and that his submissions always reflected his genuine assessment of the market.

Hayes kept his side of the bargain, and in the weeks that followed he worked his brokers and rate-setter contacts for all they were worth. Utterly confident now in his ability to move the rate, Hayes kept adding to his positions. Like a conductor, he utilized every part of his orchestra to keep Libor artificially inflated. Through ICAP he badgered Read to lean on Goodman to amend his run-through. Farr contacted his buddies at HSBC and Rabobank and asked them to help him out. Cryan required a firmer hand.

"I don't care what you have to do, all right," he told the Tullett broker in one testy exchange. "This is more important to me than fucking, you know, tickets for shit, this is like fucking real life fucking P&L. I win, you win, that's the way it works, all right."

Unfortunately for Hayes, in Cryan he had found a dud. Despite all his cajoling and threatening, there's no evidence the Tullett broker ever passed on Hayes's requests to his firm's cash desk. When Libors moved in the direction Hayes had requested, Cryan claimed the credit. If they went the other way, Cryan would ignore his calls and instruct his colleagues to tell Hayes he wasn't in the office.[9] He still happily accepted Hayes's wash payments, but it was all a sham. Over time he'd watched Hayes morph from a shy, mumbling kid into a controlling "psycho" with a "God complex", and he'd reached a point where he was willing to say whatever he thought Hayes wanted to hear just to get him off the phone.[10] Cryan, who would help organize Hayes's stag party, acknowledged stringing the trader along but denied ever actually following through on the more than 50 occasions he agreed to pass on his requests. "It's called broking," he would later explain with a smile on the stand. Cryan was acquitted of conspiring with Hayes to rig Libor at trial in London in 2016.

Despite all Hayes's efforts, yen Libor tumbled more than 6 basis points from the end of June to Aug. 10, losing him millions.

By now the trader had bigger concerns. While the heads of the investment bank recognized Hayes's money-making abilities, Ducrot was making life increasingly uncomfortable for him. The newly promoted manager ordered Hayes to fly to UBS's headquarters in Zurich to discuss the direction of the business and his future within it. Hayes saw the summons, the first of its kind, as a kick in the teeth and resented having to go. They finally came face to face in a small meeting room away from the trading floor. If Hayes was possessed of more social intelligence he may have been able to turn the situation around, but his demeanor was defensive from the start and he begrudged having to explain his worth. Ducrot had been drip-fed reports of Hayes's antics for years. The meeting was over in minutes; both sides further entrenched in their negative opinions of each other.

A few days later, still in Zurich, Hayes was sitting in the seat he'd been allocated with the junior-level rate-setters, when an e-mail from Pieri landed in his inbox. His boss was concerned about the desk's massive exposure to six-month Libor. Hayes replied casually, as he had done a hundred times before in person, that there was nothing to worry about as he was going to push Libor lower. Minutes later he got a call on his mobile, which he took outside the office, he would later testify.

"Don't ever send me an e-mail like that," Pieri shouted angrily, according to Hayes's recollection of the conversation at trial. "I could lose my job over that, you know." [11]

Hayes apologized and said he wouldn't do it again, but he was shaken by Pieri's outburst.[12] He later explained in evidence that, to his mind, Pieri knew about his methods and had never expressed any reservations. Hayes was hurt by what he perceived to be a sudden change of tone. Pieri, who was subsequently dismissed from UBS, has never been charged with an offense. Hayes felt a growing sense of bewilderment at the way he thought he was being treated by UBS.

Just when he thought things couldn't get any worse, in mid-August the trader got wind that the bank was planning on handing responsibility for setting all Libor rates to the asset & liability management desk, a separate part of the business over which Hayes had no influence whatsoever.[13] It threatened to undermine everything he'd built up so diligently. Notwithstanding the problems he had with Darin, Hayes still held some sway over the rates that UBS submitted. It was the last straw.

At the end of August, after three miserable weeks in the Zurich office, Hayes headed to France for a family holiday. After talking through his predicament with his stepfather, Hayes made up his mind to quit the bank. The infighting, the broken promises and the perceived betrayals had taken their toll. It was time for a new start. He flew back to Tokyo and handed in his notice on Sept. 2, the same week the ALM desk submitted Libor for the first time.

Chapter 11

The Call

In the weeks after Obie's encounter with his former boss in London, the CFTC's Libor investigation began to take shape. True to his word, Mocek started sending through the evidence Barclays had retrieved from its internal probe, taking the view that it was better to get out on the front foot and seek a more favorable treatment. Boxes and CDs containing e-mails, voice recordings and instant-message transcripts arrived by courier in the lead-up to Christmas 2009 and were distributed to members of the team like presents. Then, in January, Mocek came into the CFTC and gave a PowerPoint presentation. It was an early incarnation of the case for the defense.

Libor, the lawyer explained, flicking between slides, had been run without due care and attention by the BBA for years. Traders couldn't be expected to know what they could and couldn't do when there were no rules. What's more, he said, since the financial crisis had started, interbank lending had ground to a halt. Now lenders relied on central banks to prop them up. How could anyone say a bank's estimates were inaccurate when there were no correct figures to compare them with? Still, he conceded, Barclays had been shocked to identify some rogue elements and would deal with them without mercy. It was a refrain that would be wheeled out by every institution caught up in the scandal.

The rogue element Mocek was referring to was a small team of highly paid derivatives traders, mostly in their twenties, based at Barclays's

U.S. headquarters in Manhattan. Unlike Hayes and his growing coterie, who sought to influence yen Libor, the Barclays traders focused on the dollar. The group was run by a suave, aggressive India-born trader in his late thirties named Jay Merchant, who toyed with a career in tennis and used to hit balls with the Williams sisters. The traders' modus operandi was straightforward but effective. Whenever they had built a large dollar derivatives position, they would contact the individuals responsible for setting Libor at Barclays in London and tell them what numbers they wanted for different maturities. It was like ordering take-out. Some traders at the bank also called up their buddies at other institutions and asked them to make favorable submissions.[1]

The most senior rate-setter in the U.K. was a crotchety but generally compliant treasury employee named Peter Johnson, a thickset, silver-haired 50-something Englishman who understood the mantra that, at Barclays, the traders ruled the roost.

The interactions between the derivatives traders and rate-setters like Johnson reveal a lot about the hierarchies that develop within large financial institutions. Junior members of Merchant's team were wary of Johnson and would show deference to the older man, apologizing for inconveniencing him and saying in messages how much they "would appreciate any help". Merchant, whose multimillion-dollar compensation dwarfed Johnson's, followed no such protocol. In one e-mail he bypassed all pleasantries and simply wrote in a giant, screen-filling font the number he expected to see submitted by Johnson the following morning.

Two of the traders who worked with Johnson, Stylianos Contogoulas and Ryan Reich, are at the time of writing due to stand trial in London on charges of conspiracy to defraud by rigging the dollar Libor rate. Both deny the charges and say they never did anything dishonest. They also say their bosses instructed them to pass on requests to the rate-setters. The outcome of an earlier trial involving Barclays traders was subject to reporting restrictions at the time of writing.

The evidence that made its way to the seventh floor of the CFTC's headquarters that winter represented a major breakthrough, giving the team renewed impetus to go after other banks. If Barclays was trying to push Libor around so openly, it seemed likely that others were doing the same.

Still, mining the material was laborious. Members of the enforcement division spent countless hours in offices alone, slouched over their desks cataloguing documents and listening to recordings. Wall charts were drawn up showing the management structure and chain of command in different teams. The language the traders used, with its references to "IMM dates" and "reset ladders", needed to be deciphered. Even the sexual innuendos and laddish jokes, which at first offered some light relief, wore thin after a few days.

Then, in the last week of March 2010, Termine, the lawyer running the investigation day to day, brought Obie a CD that changed everything.

Commissioners rarely get involved in early-stage investigations, but that evening Obie took the recording upstairs to the ninth floor to play to Gensler and a handful of his senior lieutenants. Huddled on scuffed-up sofas and chairs in the waiting room outside the chairman's office—the only place with a CD player that worked—the atmosphere was a mixture of anticipation and frustration at this disruption to their busy schedule.

It was a telephone conversation between Johnson and his boss Mark Dearlove, Barclays's head of money markets, which had taken place during the most turbulent days of the financial crisis. No transcript of the call has ever been released, and there was no reference to it in any of the settlements that followed, but the contents are explosive.[2]

As night fell in London on Oct. 29, 2008, Dearlove, the son of the former head of Britain's Secret Intelligence Service, called Johnson on another floor of the bank's U.K. headquarters and told him, in his cut-glass British accent, that he needed to start lowering the bank's Libor submissions, particularly in sterling and dollars. The two men had known each other for more than 20 years, and Johnson, who spoke in less-refined tones, had a reputation for being stubborn. Dearlove prefaced the instruction by saying that he knew Johnson was not going to like it, but he had no choice; the order had come directly from the Bank of England and had been sanctioned by Jerry Del Missier, the executive running Barclays's trading operations at the time.

One CFTC employee present when the tape was played said the discussion, which lasted less than five minutes, was so unambiguous that it seemed like the two men knew they were being recorded—as if, on some level, they knew the conversation might be preserved and they needed to cover their asses.

What the CFTC officials heard that afternoon, gathered around an aging portable CD player, was the evidence that would break open the case. Here was a Barclays manager laying out how the bank planned to falsify its Libor submissions in order to salvage its reputation. What's more, the order seemed to come from the bank's executive suite, which in turn was responding to an instruction from the Bank of England. It was the smoking gun that would ultimately derail the careers of one of the most revered bankers of his generation and the man touted as the next Governor of the Bank of England.

Beyond a brief memo written by Barclays CEO Bob Diamond (at the time he was head of Barclays Capital, the investment bank) and published two years later, the recording is the closest thing to proof that bankers during the crisis were being told to doctor Libor by the U.K.'s central bank as part of a last-ditch attempt to rescue the financial system from total collapse.

The CFTC would spend the next few months trying to piece together the chain of events that had led Dearlove to make that crucial call in 2008. The story they uncovered began a few hours earlier, in Diamond's office in London. It was a fevered, precarious time in which everything was at stake and desperate measures, of the type that are rarely admitted publicly, were being considered.

■ ■ ■

Robert Edward Diamond Jr., Red to his friends, was born on July 27, 1951, the second of nine children. His parents, Anne and Robert Edward Sr., were Irish Catholic high school teachers who bestowed on their children a strong sense of civic duty but few of the connections and privileges that can help ease the path to success in high finance. The family lived in Concord, Massachusetts, an affluent, picture-postcard town where the first battles of the American Revolution were fought and the novel *Little Women* was set. Diamond walked to Concord-Carlisle High School every morning, where his dad was the superintendent. Five-foot-10 and stocky, he was a star linebacker until he injured his knee in college. Sport provided an outlet for a fierce competitive streak.

Diamond graduated with honors from Colby College in Maine before finishing first in his MBA class at the University of Connecticut.

After brief spells as a lecturer and an analyst at a surgical equipment company, Diamond joined Morgan Stanley in 1979, the same year Gensler started working at Goldman Sachs. He was hired to help introduce computers to the investment bank's trading floor but quickly switched to trading bonds.

Diamond's entry into Wall Street may have been late, but he wasted no time once he got there. He became a managing director before his 35th birthday, and by the time he left Morgan Stanley for Credit Suisse First Boston in 1992, he was running the bank's European and Asian bond-trading operations. Diamond then moved his young family to Japan to become the Swiss bank's chairman, president and CEO for Asia. He was soon promoted to head of fixed income and currencies globally and given a seat on the executive board in New York.

In 1996, Barclays CEO Martin Taylor, an Eton and Oxford-educated former journalist, hired the 45-year-old Diamond to come to London and run the lender's securities and investment division. By then fixed income, currencies and commodities, or FICC as it's known in the industry, was driving profits at the bulge-bracket investment banks and Diamond was a rising star. One of his first moves was to sell the equities and merchant banking operations to concentrate on debt capital markets. That decision paid off when the dot-com bubble burst, equities plummeted and companies, governments and households increasingly turned to debt to fund themselves.

Taylor, now a policymaker at the Bank of England, went on to regret Diamond's appointment, claiming that his success came at the expense of the 325-year-old bank's reputation and was built on a disregard for internal controls. According to Taylor, Diamond had gone to Barclays's credit committee in the spring of 1998 to ask for a fivefold increase in exposure to Russian counterparties. "I cut the request back by roughly half," Taylor wrote later. "They were disappointed, but within a few months the situation in Russia had deteriorated so much that no one was arguing about the credit ceiling."[3]

When Russia defaulted on its debt that August, Taylor knew the bank was facing a serious loss, but he didn't realize how much. On a call with his treasurer, he learned that the bank's traders had got around the credit committee's restrictions by falsely marking some Russian counterparties as Swiss or American.

"We looked reckless, and our share price suffered serious damage. The traders were fired," Taylor wrote. "Their leader maintained that he had known nothing about what was going on. He felt terrible. He loved Barclays."

Taylor left the bank soon after the episode, uncomfortable with the direction Diamond and the board members were taking the business. Meanwhile, Barclays Capital, as the investment bank was now known, thrived. In 1997, Diamond's first year in charge, the business made a profit of £248 million, about 14 percent of the group total. Ten years later, in 2007, it returned £2.3 billion and accounted for about a third of all profit. Over the same period Barclays Capital's assets ballooned from £135 billion to £840 billion.

By the end of 2006, shares in Barclays had risen threefold to 657 pence. The directors couldn't have been happier. John Varley, who took over as CEO in September 2004, said in a 2007 interview with Diamond's college newspaper: "When he joined Barclays, which was about ten years ago, I think that what we had then was an underperforming, subscale investment banking capability. And what we have today is an outperforming world leader. That's quite a transformation in ten years. And Bob has personally led that."

Diamond's arrival in the U.K. coincided with the advance of American firms in the capital, and his success mirrored the City of London's in the decade after Tony Blair's New Labour government swept into power promising "things can only get better". The light-touch regulatory environment created by the Big Bang reforms of 1986 lured American powerhouses like Goldman Sachs, Citigroup, JPMorgan and Merrill Lynch. They brought with them a new professionalism and an increased appetite for risk. Twelve-hour days replaced boozy lunches, and prestigious British names like Schroders, Smith New Court, Barings and Cazenove were taken over, supplanted or crushed by the competition. Private partnerships, in which executives were on the line for losses at their firms, were replaced by public companies whose shareholders bore the brunt of any mistakes.

Hedge funds and private equity, previously bit-part players in global financial markets, became responsible for bigger and bigger pots of capital. Many set up base in the swanky streets of Mayfair. At the same time, emerging markets like Russia and India were experiencing unprecedented growth. With its ready infrastructure and convenient time zone, London was a natural conduit between East and West.

Powering the financial boom years was an ethos of unbridled financial innovation. Derivatives markets globally jumped from $80 trillion to $592 trillion between 1998 and 2008,[4] accompanied by what turned out to be a misguided belief that the complex financial instruments served to disperse rather than concentrate risk. Between 2003 and 2008, bonuses in the City rose from £3.3 billion to £11.6 billion.[5]

With a 1,000-watt smile, a townhouse in Belgravia and a box at Chelsea football club's Stamford Bridge stadium, Diamond rode the crest of the wave. Barclays started sponsoring the Premiership, England's soccer franchise, in 2001. At the end of each season, Diamond walked onto the pitch to hand over the trophy, sometimes to his beloved Chelsea. While others shunned the limelight, he posed beaming for newspaper profiles.

In the spring of 2007, Barclays launched an audacious all-share bid for Dutch lender ABN Amro. With a market valuation of €70 billion ($79 billion), it was to be the biggest bank acquisition in history. As it transpired, a consortium led by RBS trumped Barclays with an all-cash offer. It turned out to be a lucky escape. RBS and its partners had hugely overpaid for a bank stuffed with toxic assets just as the markets turned. They would pay dearly for their folly.[6]

As the financial crisis deepened, Barclays, like all large banks, grappled with the problem of Libor. While some of its rivals seemed content to submit figures that were completely fabricated, Johnson and his fellow rate-setters at Barclays shared an almost quaint desire to reflect the truth. Between Sept. 1, 2007, and Dec. 31, 2008, Barclays's three-month dollar submissions were in or equal to the top four of the 16 contributing banks 89 percent of the time—that is, they were closer to reality than their peers.

Frustrated at the effect that was having on their reputation, employees at the bank alerted regulators and the BBA to the problem of lowballing on more than two dozen occasions over the period.[7] What they failed to mention was that senior managers at Barclays were ordering them to do the same thing. Internally there was a tug of war between wanting to submit accurate rates and needing to avoid the stigma of always being an outlier. In the end, the bank's approach to setting Libor during the crisis can be summarized by a November 2007 e-mail sent by Dearlove to the bank's rate-setters: "Thanks for remaining pragmatic but at the upper end."

In the summer of 2008, Diamond moved his family back to the U.S. after the youngest of his three children finished school. Diamond's mission was to help Barclays find the missing piece of the jigsaw: a foothold in the U.S. Within three months an opportunity presented itself that nobody could have foreseen—another example of the uncanny timing that had marked his career.

On Monday, Sept. 15, Lehman Brothers was declared bankrupt. The previous week Barclays had scrambled to buy the whole business, but the U.K. government and financial regulator refused to sign off on the acquisition.[8] As it turned out, a senior official in the U.S. Treasury called Varley on the Monday brokering a deal for Lehman's U.S. business—the only part it really coveted—for next to nothing. It was a much better outcome and, within a year, Barclays had reported a $4 billion gain on the trade.[9] Diamond Bob had done it again.

■ ■ ■

Six weeks after the Lehman deal closed, on Oct. 29, 2008, Diamond was sitting in his office, among the Red Sox pennants and Chelsea FC photographs, when the deputy governor of the Bank of England called. There was nothing unusual about that: As the executive responsible for financial stability, Paul Tucker was in regular contact with many senior banking executives, especially during the crisis.[10]

Still, Diamond and Tucker were particularly close. E-mails between the two men reveal a chummy relationship that later raised some eyebrows among politicians. When Tucker, a brusque, jowly man, was made deputy governor, Diamond sent him a note saying "Well done, man. I am really, really proud of you." Tucker replied: "Thanks so much Bob, you've been an absolute brick."[11]

Tucker was calling to relay concerns within the U.K. government about Barclays's ability to weather the storm. Three weeks earlier, over the course of a now infamous weekend in the history of the financial crisis, executives from banks including RBS, Standard Chartered and Lloyds Banking Group had met with regulators and members of the U.K. Treasury to formulate a plan to save the British banking system. After 48 hours in a fetid, pizza-strewn Treasury conference room, the group emerged, blinking, early on the morning of Monday, Oct. 13, to announce that RBS and Lloyds would be bailed out to the tune of £37 billion.[12]

One party notable by its absence was Barclays, which steadfastly refused to countenance taking government money and losing its independence. Varley spent the weekend holed up in his office in Canary Wharf ignoring the government's increasingly strident requests to join them, while Marcus Agius, the bank's slender, patrician chairman, was at an emergency International Monetary Fund (IMF) meeting in Washington. They believed that if they had turned up at the Treasury that weekend there was a strong chance they too would have been dragged into state ownership.

Barclays executives felt they were in an existential battle, pitted against forces intent on taking control of the bank. King at the Bank of England advocated the model adopted by Sweden in 1992 and later by the U.S. in its Troubled Asset Relief Program (TARP), which involved forcing everyone to take state aid, thereby removing the stigma attached to any specific firms. Indeed, when King had persuaded Lloyds CEO Eric Daniels to agree to its bailout, he had assured him that Barclays would also be on board.[13]

Within the government, Business Minister Shriti Vadera, a former UBS banker, tried to convince Barclays to take the medicine, arguing it was better to resolve the situation now than come back begging in two months. Over the weekend before the bailout announcement, the BBC, led with a story, citing unnamed sources, that said four banks had agreed to take the money. One of them was Barclays.[14]

In fact, Barclays was given six months to come up with additional capital, along with the more Asia-focused HSBC and Standard Chartered. Barclays's confidence in its ability to remain self-sufficient rested on the fact that its exposure to the mortgage market was relatively limited compared with the likes of RBS, Northern Rock and HBOS. It also argued it had better access to funding than its peers as skittish investors exercised a flight to quality.[15]

Executives set off on an investor tour, promising shareholders they would streamline the business, cut dividends and suspend bonuses, but their assurances failed to stop the rot that was now spreading indiscriminately across the financial sector. Barclays shares fell 11 percent to

177 pence in the two weeks after the RBS and Lloyds bailouts were announced. They had started the month at 315 pence.

The decision not to take government funds had left the bank severely exposed. Prices on Barclays credit default swaps, essentially bets on the likelihood the bank would default on its debts, went through the roof. The loudest alarm bells came from its own Libor submissions, which authorities at the time still took to be an accurate indicator of stress. On Oct. 20, Barclays estimated it would need to pay an interest rate of 4.25 percent to borrow U.S. dollars for three months, compared with 3.90 percent for Lloyds and 4.05 percent for HSBC. By the end of the week, that had fallen to 3.95 percent versus 3.45 percent for both Lloyds and HSBC. It was a repeat of the previous August, when articles appeared in *Bloomberg* and elsewhere questioning why Barclays was paying more than everyone else to borrow cash.

In Westminster, senior civil servants, the unelected mandarins of power, were growing increasingly nervous. A series of e-mails between Tucker and Jeremy Heywood, then private secretary to Prime Minister Gordon Brown, sent in the days leading up to Tucker's call with Diamond, reveal the government had two principal concerns: Why were U.K. borrowing costs, as reflected by sterling Libor, not falling as fast as dollar Libor when the government had just fired a £40 billion bazooka at British banks? And what the hell was going on at Barclays?[16]

Tucker, whose office was on the ground floor of the Bank of England, laid it out plainly for Diamond. Treasury is worried that Barclays can't access money, he said; and that could have real repercussions in your pursuit of investment.

Diamond was incensed. It was bullshit, he replied. We're one of the only banks actually able to get money beyond overnight at the moment. When Tucker asked him why Barclays's Libor numbers were higher than everyone else's, Diamond said it was because it was the only bank being even vaguely honest about its borrowing costs.[17]

Diamond had a point. RBS and Lloyds had continued to post lower figures than Barclays even as they were bailed out. A year later, King elicited a sharp intake of breath when he revealed at a Treasury Select Committee hearing that the two banks had secretly been given £62 billion in emergency loans in October 2008 after they were frozen out of the money markets altogether.[18] For at least a month, then, the Bank of

England watched the banks submit Libor figures that were demonstrably false.[19]

That's not how Westminster sees it, Tucker replied. They're just looking at Libor and seeing that you're highest again. The more Tucker spoke, the more anxious Diamond became. The call could not have come at a worse time. At that moment, 3,000 miles away, a cadre of senior Barclays executives and their advisers from Goldman Sachs were sitting in an air-conditioned suite in Doha with members of the Qatari royal family trying desperately to agree to a deal that would save the bank from the clutches of the British government.

Barclays needed at least £6 billion, but every time it thought it was closing in on a deal, the oil-rich nation raised some new issue. The $170 billion Qatar Investment Authority fund had an existing stake in Barclays, but there was no guarantee Sheikh Hamad bin Jassim bin Jabr al-Thani, the mercurial Qatari prime minister, would reach into his pockets again. If he got wind of the government's concerns, it could put the whole thing in jeopardy.

Diamond was convinced that factions in the British establishment and among Barclays's rivals were spreading rumors that the bank was in trouble. If the Qatar deal fell through, they had nowhere else to turn. He told Tucker that a deal was on the table that would put this sorry episode to bed. They just needed a bit more time.

What Tucker said next has been the subject of intense scrutiny and speculation because it gets to the heart of whether the Bank of England permitted, or even ordered, Barclays to lowball Libor. No recording of the conversation was made. The only log was a memo produced by Diamond and e-mailed to Varley and Del Missier at 2:19 p.m. the following day. Diamond's decision to send the note at all was significant because he rarely wrote memos. The last paragraph read:

> "Mr Tucker stated the level of calls he was receiving from Whitehall were 'senior' and that while he was certain we did not need advice, that it did not always need to be the case that we appeared as high as we have recently."[20]

The U.K. authorities had every reason to want banks to supress their submissions. Falling Libors would be a sign that the measures they had put in place to tackle the crisis were having an effect, which could have helped calm the markets. Privately, at least one director at the Bank of England felt Tucker was justified in issuing the order if it meant buying Barclays more time to avoid nationalization, potentially saving U.K. taxpayers billions of pounds.

In other words, the end justified the means. It would not be the first time the Bank of England had cast aside normal standards of propriety in the interest of what it perceived to be the greater good. When property prices crashed in the so-called secondary banking crisis of the mid-1970s, then-Governor Gordon Richardson propped up ailing banks with a raft of loans that were kept secret from the public in an attempt to contain the problem until markets recovered. It worked, and, when his career came to an end two decades later, Richardson described it privately as his crowning achievement.

For his part, Diamond has always maintained that he never took Tucker's words as a direct order to start lowballing Libor.[21] That impression, he says, began on a call with his most trusted lieutenant later that day.

■ ■ ■

Jerry Del Missier joined Barclays the year after Diamond, and any credit Diamond deserves for the rapid growth of the investment bank must be shared with the small, intense Canadian. As head of markets, Del Missier oversaw the expansion of the operation that contributed so much to group profits over the next decade. As one board member puts it, Diamond was the salesman, Del Missier was the brains and Rich Ricci, an executive who held a number of senior roles, was the enforcer. Senior executives at the bank describe Del Missier as sharp, unflashy and ruthless. Like Diamond, he bled Barclays. At the end of a two-week trekking trip to the top of the Mera Peak in the Himalayas in 2007, he planted a blue and white flag emblazoned with the bank's logo.[22]

Shortly after Diamond got off the phone with Tucker, he called Del Missier in New York and relayed the contents of the conversation. Del Missier remembers the discussion unequivocally: "He said that he had a conversation with Mr. Tucker of the Bank of England, that the Bank of England was getting pressure from Whitehall around Barclays—the health of Barclays—as a result of Libor rates—that we should get our Libor rates down, and that we should not be outliers."[23]

Because Diamond's conversation with Del Missier wasn't recorded, there is no way of knowing exactly what was said. One senior U.S. investigator assigned to the Barclays case says in the end it doesn't really matter. Whether Diamond issued a direct order or simply restated Tucker's line about not always needing to "appear as high", the effect was the same. "If the president says the word shit, you squat and ask questions later," the investigator puts it bluntly. It is a cruel twist that Del Missier's relationship with Diamond is what enmeshed him in the scandal: Libor submissions were actually the responsibility of the bank's treasury department, a separate unit run by a British executive named Jonathan Stone, but Diamond's closeness with Del Missier meant it was the Canadian he contacted first.

Later that day, Del Missier called Dearlove in Canary Wharf and told him to start lowering the bank's dollar and sterling Libor submissions. There was no pushback. The conversation was over in minutes. The die was cast. When he got off the phone, Dearlove called Johnson and relayed the instruction—the call that was now in the hands of the giddy CFTC in Washington.

When the CFTC investigators cross-referenced the Libor figures with the recordings, they saw that the instruction had been followed. On Oct. 30, the day after Tucker's call, Barclays' three-month U.S. dollar Libor submission fell 60 basis points to 3.4 percent—the biggest one-day percentage fall in more than a month. The following day it went down another 20 basis points. The sterling figures followed a similar pattern.

On Friday, Oct. 31, 2008, after another round of intense negotiations in Doha, Barclays announced it had secured a £7.3 billion capital injection from the Qataris and the Abu Dhabi sovereign wealth fund, assuring its independence.[24] When the European Central Bank and the Bank of England slashed interest rates a week later, Libor plummeted across the board. The crisis had been averted.

One individual raised concerns that what the bank was doing was wrong: Johnson, the veteran cash trader, who would later plead guilty to helping traders rig Libor by nudging the bank's submissions up and down for years.[25] In an e-mail to Barclays's head of compliance, he wrote:

"As per the telephonic communication today with Mark Dearlove. I have been requested to reduce the Sterling Libor rates to be more in line with the 'Pack'. As I understand it this is an instruction by either senior management and/or the Bank of England. I voiced my views as below but as such will comply with the request...but it should be noted that this will be breaking the BBA rules."

For Johnson, it was one thing to move his submissions up and down by a fraction of a basis point here and there to suit traders' positions. The rate was an estimate anyway so who was to say that, within a given range, one was more accurate than the other? What his managers were asking him to do was knowingly lie by suggesting the bank's borrowing costs were 30 basis points or more lower than they were. That was having a real effect—on savers with money tied up in accounts with interest payments linked to Libor, for example. Compliance did not follow up on the issue.

Chapter 12

Crossing the Street

C rossing the street, in Washington parlance, is the act of taking a civil case to the Justice Department to launch a criminal investigation. From the CFTC's red-awninged headquarters on the outskirts of the city center to the DOJ's shabby Bond Building in the middle of town it's more like a 20-minute walk, past the glass-fronted citadels of the International Monetary Fund and the World Bank on Pennsylvania Avenue, through Lafayette Square and the tourists taking photos outside the White House lawn, to the corner of 14th Street and New York Avenue.

For the CFTC it was a pretty unusual journey to make. The two authorities had worked together—on Enron in 2002 and the natural gas price manipulation cases, for example—but the default position for regulators was to hold onto cases for dear life lest the Justice Department swoop in and take over, or worse, claim the credit. Libor was particularly · sensitive because the CFTC had started pursuing it back in 2008, when no one else had the curiosity—or the sense of right and wrong—to investigate.

After hearing the Barclays tape, though, the CFTC knew it had to call in the feds. The DOJ has the power to indict individuals, set up a grand jury and, ultimately, close down businesses and send people to jail. If managers at the British bank were ordering the lowballing of Libor and traders were pushing the rate around for profit, that potentially constituted fraud, which warranted steeper punishments than a civil authority alone could dole out.

The CFTC's point man in the Justice Department's fraud section was a tall, genial, gray-bearded attorney named Robertson Park, who was raised in the shadow of the Brooklyn Bridge and studied at Antioch School of Law in Washington. There he was thrust into public advocacy, working on behalf of disenfranchised citizens from his first semester. After a short spell in private practice, Park joined the Justice Department in 1992 and had been there ever since. One afternoon in early April 2010, he was sitting at his desk when Obie called. The two men had worked the natural gas cases together and still met up for the occasional beer.

"Rob, drop what you're doing and listen to this," Obie said. Holding the handset of his phone up to the speakers on his desk, he played the Barclays recording. When it was over, Park's first words were "holy shit".

A week later, a handful of enforcement people from the CFTC were sitting around a U-shaped table in a tatty conference room on the third floor of the Bond Building with half a dozen officials from Justice. The walls of the grandiosely named Seal Room were decorated with crests, some wood but most plastic, of the various U.S. government and military agencies. In one corner the ceiling tiles had been removed to accommodate a collection of aging flags on poles weirdly too tall for the room.

By now, day-to-day responsibility for Libor at the CFTC rested with the agency's odd couple: Lowe, the reserved supervisor with the slow, deliberate delivery; and Termine, the scrappy, younger case manager from the New Orleans DA's office who stood several inches shorter than her boss and became louder and more animated as she talked. Over the next few hours they presented the evidence and laid out where they were with the case. Aside from Barclays, none of the banks had been particularly forthcoming, they explained. Some had completely ignored the agency's requests for information.

On the DOJ side, Park had invited his boss, the newly appointed head of the fraud section, Denis McInerney, who was there with his deputy and a handful of other attorneys. None of them knew anything about Libor and were astounded to learn how pervasive it was: how swaps, loans and mortgages taken out by companies, federal and local governments and ordinary people were pegged to it; and how trillions of dollars of contracts globally depended on where it was set each day.

Fraud is one of 10 sections that sit under the umbrella of the Justice Department's criminal division. It is the principal litigator for white-collar crime in the U.S., often working in collaboration with the 93 U.S. Attorneys' Offices across the country. Two years after the financial crisis, it was going through a rough time.

The American public expected the high-rolling Wall Street executives who ran the banks to pay for their deeds. It was not simply a case of recklessness and greed. There was mounting evidence that some firms had systematically and knowingly lied about the value of their mortgage assets. By repackaging crappy, subprime home loans into mortgage-backed securities and flogging them to unsuspecting investors as AAA rated, there was a case to be made that the bankers had committed mortgage fraud and should be criminally prosecuted.

But going after bank executives was not as easy as it sounded and, as the DOJ liked to point out, there were other considerations.[1] The European debt crisis, which started in Greece and Portugal, was now churning up markets globally. Lenders still relied on government loans and record low interest rates to survive. Justice was obliged to consider the collateral consequences of any enforcement action it took, and it argued that prosecuting banks and their executives would have a destabilizing, maybe even a catastrophic, effect on firms employing hundreds of thousands of people, as well as the broader economy.[2]

The decision not to prosecute rested largely with one man: the head of the criminal division, Lanny Breuer. Breuer was raised in Queens, New York, the son of German and Austrian holocaust survivors. He made his name in the 1990s defending Bill Clinton from a string of scandals culminating in the impeachment proceedings in 1998. Before and after his spell as special counsel to the president, Breuer was a partner at Washington law firm Covington & Burling, where he worked alongside Eric Holder.[3] The century-old firm specializes in representing banks and corporations accused of financial crimes, something critics argue colored Breuer's decision-making. Its clients have included Citigroup, Fannie Mae, Bank of America and Wells Fargo.

Following his election in 2008, President Obama named Holder Attorney General—the most senior law enforcement officer in the country—and Breuer head of the criminal division reporting to him. Former managers in the division complain Breuer was controlling and risk-averse. Cases they felt were solid were dropped because of what they describe as an institutional fear of failure. Short, with cropped hair, glasses and a nasally voice, Breuer courted journalists and closely monitored how his decisions played out in the press.

If Breuer was fixated with the media, that was understandable. When he arrived, the criminal division was mired in scandal and infighting. The previous October, Ted Stevens, the 84-year-old Republican Senator for Alaska, was convicted of failing to report gifts, namely renovations to a house he owned. Stevens's prosecution, which came at the climax of his re-election campaign, was part of a broader probe into corruption in Alaska by the criminal division's public integrity section. The four-year investigation was a success, leading to nine convictions and exposing a network of public officials who routinely took bribes and called themselves "The Corrupt Bastards Club". By aiming for the veteran senator, however, the agency had badly overreached.

The case against Stevens, a popular and respected figure who had served more than four decades in office, was flimsy. Five weeks after his prosecution it emerged that Justice officials had suppressed potentially exculpatory evidence. In April 2009, a few months after taking office, Holder withdrew the indictment, removed some of the prosecutors from their posts and ordered an independent investigation into the handling of the case. It was too late for Stevens, who had already lost his bid for re-election and was killed in a plane crash a year later.[4]

When Libor turned up on the Justice Department's doorstep in the spring of 2010, it represented more than just another white-collar case. For Breuer and the bosses of the criminal division, it was an opportunity to turn the tables. Banks that sat on the Libor panels such as Citigroup, Barclays, UBS and RBS were among those that had escaped prosecution for their part in causing the financial crisis. Coming down hard on them now would go some way toward demonstrating that the government wasn't afraid to hold big money to account. That the CFTC had done a lot of the groundwork was an added bonus.

Within a week of the Seal Room meeting, the DOJ formally agreed to launch its own investigation. Park was given responsibility for leading the probe into Barclays. Two junior attorneys, Nicole Sprinzen and Luke

Marsh,[5] were also assigned to the case, and from a small bank of desks on the third floor of the Bond Building, the three of them set to work.

■ ■ ■

On the other side of the Atlantic, in a waterside office block in Canary Wharf, the FSA remained resolutely disengaged. Libor may have been set in London and overseen by the BBA, but the U.K. regulator demonstrated no desire to get involved in an expensive and potentially messy investigation if it didn't have to. Since the fall of 2008, its role had been little more than a glorified postal service, receiving evidence from the banks and sending it on to the CFTC. There was so little input from the FSA that CFTC investigators wondered if they even looked at it.

The FSA was formed in 1997 by then-Chancellor of the Exchequer Gordon Brown as part of an overhaul of the way financial businesses were regulated in the U.K. Brown believed that a light-touch approach to supervising the banks would foster greater efficiency and creativity, and for a decade it worked. The financial sector boomed, tax revenues soared and prosecutions for malfeasance went down. Then the crisis hit and everyone wondered what the hell the government was thinking giving so much freedom to the bankers.

Now, with a general election scheduled for May 6, 2010, the FSA was fighting for its life. The Conservative Party, which had a big lead in the polls, had issued a policy paper threatening to abolish the FSA and grant more power for regulating the financial system to the Bank of England. The FSA building became darker for a spell each day when the sun passed behind One Canada Square, the 50-story skyscraper across the street. By the spring of 2010, it seemed there was a constant shadow hanging over it.

Feeling her way in the dark was the FSA's Head of Enforcement, Margaret Cole, a small woman with short sandy hair and a permanently harassed expression. Cole, who was brought up in a working-class family in the north of England, had joined the FSA in 2005 after making a name for herself in private practice helping retrieve assets for pension holders swindled by the late media tycoon Robert Maxwell before he fell off the back of his yacht and drowned.

Obie had been trying to get Cole to take a more active role in Libor for a while in the hope she could secure greater cooperation from the recalcitrant banks in London, but philosophically the FSA saw the world very differently to the U.S. agency. When evidence emerged that the Bank of England may have pushed Barclays to lowball its Libor submissions during the crisis, the U.K. regulator had difficulty understanding what all the fuss was about. Former managers at the agency argued that desperate times had called for desperate measures. And besides, in typically British fashion, it was deemed unseemly for the regulator to hold the central bank's feet to the coals.

It didn't help that the Bank of England's Paul Tucker sat on the board of directors of the FSA. Tucker was a strong character and an esteemed figure in the British establishment with close ties to many senior bank executives. When Cole herself was catapulted to the board following a string of departures at the regulator after the general election, her immediate goal was to keep her head down and stay out of trouble. Questioning the propriety of the potential future governor of the Bank of England would not have been a great career move. In the end the FSA never formally interviewed Tucker as part of its Libor investigation.[6]

It was only when evidence emerged in the spring of 2010 showing derivatives traders nudging the rate up and down for profit that the FSA began to consider taking a more active role. By then, the Conservatives were in power and the regulator was in meltdown.[7] A month after the election, as George Osborne prepared to give his maiden Mansion House speech as Chancellor of the Exchequer, Hector Sants, the head of the FSA, threatened to leave. He was persuaded to stay, but his head of risk, Sally Dewar, quit and a few weeks after that Jon Pain, head of supervision, also walked away leaving a chasm at the top of the organization.

By the summer, the Libor investigation was proceeding with little involvement from the U.K. authorities. It may have stayed that way if it wasn't for a misstep by one of Barclays's external lawyers.

When the bank was lining up law firms to advise it on the Libor investigation at the end of 2008, McDermott Will & Emery, a well-regarded but mid-tier Chicago outfit, was not the obvious choice. As one of the world's largest financial institutions, the British bank might have been expected to opt for one of the elite firms whose attorneys went to the top schools and had the best connections. However, McDermott had something the Cravath Swaine & Moores and Freshfield Bruckhaus Deringers of the world didn't: Greg Mocek.

Confident and charismatic, with a slow southern drawl and a ready smile, Mocek pitched himself to Barclays as the best man to get them out of the mess they were in. As the former head of enforcement at the CFTC—Obie's predecessor—he was uniquely placed to deal with the agency. On top of that, he had a good relationship with Cole at the FSA in London.

Cole and Mocek had become friendly during their years as counterparts at their respective agencies, meeting up at the FSA's annual conference for senior enforcement officials in Wilton Park, a secluded country estate outside London, or over dinner when Cole was in Washington.

Mocek is married to Avery Miller, an Emmy-winning television news producer for ABC News. Former colleagues say he shares with his wife an aptitude for spin and an acute sense of how stories will play out in the media. When Barclays unearthed the recording linking the Bank of England to Libor lowballing, he saw the opportunity immediately.

On a summer evening in 2010, six months or so after Mocek gave his presentation at the CFTC, he called Cole on her mobile phone. The tone was friendly, but the message was clear: We've both heard the Barclays tape. You need to consider the political ramifications of this. If this gets out it will be highly embarrassing for Barclays, for the Bank of England and for the FSA.

It was, according to several people with direct knowledge of the matter, the start of a campaign to get the FSA to suppress the case against Barclays.

A few days later, Mocek called Cole again. When she didn't reply, he left a voice message. When Mocek called a third time, she snapped. Cole considered it inappropriate that Mocek would use their relationship to try to sway the case. "I don't think I should be speaking to you anymore," she told him and hung up.

Mocek's friendship with Cole only went so far. The mounting evidence against the bank made it impossible for the FSA to stand aside any longer. After calling Obie at the CFTC to vent her anger, Cole contacted Barclays's in-house counsel and demanded they remove Mocek from the case. Within 24 hours, McDermott Will & Emery had been dropped and replaced by Sullivan & Cromwell. Barclays and its new counsel held a wipe-the-slate-clean meeting with the CFTC, Justice and the FSA on May 6, 2010. Finally, more than two years after it was alerted to the problem, the FSA formally launched an investigation into Libor.

With Justice and the FSA onboard, the Libor investigation entered a new phase. The CFTC sent letters to the 16 banks on the dollar Libor panel, compelling them to hand over evidence and make staff available for interviews. It also instructed them to appoint external law firms to undertake investigations into Libor rigging and report back with their findings by the end of the year.

It is a bizarre and controversial feature of the current regulatory system that banks are effectively given responsibility to investigate themselves because the authorities cannot afford to do it. Whenever a bank is instructed to undertake an internal investigation, it decides the parameters for inquiry, the law firms that will carry it out and how much it will pay them. There are no restrictions on who the bank's executives can appoint, meaning they often hire firms with which they have longstanding commercial relationships. When Barclays sold its Barclays Global Investors (BGI) fund management unit for $13.5 billion that summer, it appointed Clifford Chance and Sullivan & Cromwell as its legal advisers on the transaction. The same two firms were hired to work on the Libor probe. Such arrangements are common and there is no suggestion of a conflict of interest.

Barclays would later report that its internal investigation into Libor involved reviewing 22 million documents, interviewing 75 people and listening to more than 1 million audio files. The total cost was £100 million—more than half the CFTC's entire annual budget. Libor was just one of hundreds of probes carried out by the CFTC each year and, with dozens of banks in its purview, it had no choice but to delegate.

For the big-ticket law firms that got in on the act it was a bonanza. All 16 banks on the dollar panel hired at least two firms, one in the U.S. and one in the U.K., to deal with the different authorities. There were lawyers advising the banks' executives, lawyers representing the implicated individuals, lawyers who specialized in fraud, lawyers who focused on antitrust, lawyers for every jurisdiction. As the investigation progressed, it was not unusual for bank employees to be accompanied on their interviews with the authorities by as many as six attorneys, all being paid an hourly rate.

The banks understood it was an expense worth bearing. By hiring armies of the best lawyers in the world, they could effectively clog up an investigation, arguing over the admissibility of every piece of evidence, the ground rules for every interview and the meaning of every clause.

One bank, to the chagrin of investigators, was proving particularly unforthcoming. Eighteen months after the CFTC's first request for information in October 2008, UBS had supplied the agency with almost nothing. Swiss privacy laws are among the strongest in the world, and UBS's lawyers insisted that passing transcripts and recordings of conversations involving Swiss employees to foreign authorities would run counter to those laws. They also challenged the agency's jurisdiction to subpoena UBS traders in Europe and Asia.

If the CFTC was going to break down the walls, it would have to try a different approach. On the last weekend in June, Obie took an overnight flight from Washington to Bern with a secret weapon—Phyllis Cela, one of the agency's longest-serving and best-connected attorneys. From the airport they took a taxi to an office block overlooking an expressway that housed Finma, the Swiss Financial Market Supervisory Authority.

Notwithstanding the huge geographical areas that they supervise and the trillion-dollar markets they oversee, the white-collar enforcement community is surprisingly small and close knit. Cela, who was close to retiring after almost three decades at the agency, was the CFTC's representative on IOSCO, something akin to a trade body. Once a year delegates from dozens of regulators around the world descend on a different city to participate in panel discussions and meet up with old friends. In 2007 it was Mumbai, in 2008 Paris, in 2009 Tel Aviv. It was on one such trip that Cela had met Urs Zulauf, Finma's general counsel and the man whose office they were sitting in now.

Obie and Cela explained that they needed Finma's help getting UBS to cooperate with the investigation. By now the Justice Department had also started investigating the Swiss bank for helping U.S. citizens avoid taxes. Zulauf didn't need reminding that UBS's infractions were reflecting badly on the Swiss banking sector, and, by association, its regulator. He told his guests to leave it with him and showed them to the

door. Shortly afterwards a compromise was reached between the regulator and its largest bank. UBS documents would be passed to the U.S.
agencies via Finma, thereby circumventing the privacy laws. There were
still some restrictions on what they could procure—conversations held
solely between employees in Switzerland were still protected. But it was
a turning point in the investigation. Hayes knew nothing about it, but
the invisible force field that had been protecting him and his partners
was slowly losing its power.

Chapter 13

"What the Fuck Kind of Bank Is This?"

ayes walked through the sliding glass doors of the Shin-Marunouchi skyscraper for the first time as a Citigroup employee in December 2009.

It wasn't just the $3 million signing bonus that had lured him away from UBS. The promise of a fresh start at one of the world's biggest banks, with him center stage in its aggressive expansion into the Asian interest-rate derivatives market, had proved too tempting an offer to resist.

As he rode up to the trading floor in the elevator that winter morning, Hayes had every reason to expect a bright future. Bouncing back from its bailout, Citigroup had repaid much of the $45 billion it had taken after suffering crippling losses linked to the collapse of the U.S. subprime-mortgage market. Rather than being humbled by the experience, the firm saw the credit crisis as an opportunity to revive its fortunes. After Lehman Brothers collapsed in 2008, Citigroup scooped up more than a dozen of its best traders to spearhead a push into interest-rate derivatives. Rates was one of the only areas of banking making any money amid the chaos, and one where Citigroup had long been a laggard.

The bank's chief hire was Andrew Morton, a Canadian former academic renowned for developing a groundbreaking mathematical model to price interest-rate swaps. In the year since he joined as the head of G-10 rates, risk treasury and finance, the one-time professor at the University of Illinois at Chicago had overseen a rapid expansion of the bank's derivatives-trading operations.

Most of Morton's hires had been in Europe and the U.S. and now he wanted to replicate the model in Asia. Hayes, who had singlehandedly transformed the yen swaps market from a boring backwater into a lucrative business for UBS, seemed a perfect addition to his growing stable of hot young traders. In three years he had made the Swiss bank a staggering $300 million.

Morton tapped his former acolyte at Lehman, Chris Cecere, to head the team in Asia and set aside millions of dollars for him to lure the best talent. Hayes was their round-one pick. After persuading him to join, Cecere boasted to colleagues that he'd found "a real fucking animal", who had 40 percent of the short-end yen swaps market sewn up and "knows everybody on the street".[1]

During his mandatory three-month leave, Hayes had already begun laying the groundwork for the next chapter of his career. Rather than kick back and relax, he flew around the world meeting hedge fund managers and investors and introducing himself to future colleagues who might be of use to him down the line. He would rather have been at his desk trading, but Hayes hoped the connections he made would open up new flows of information. An added bonus was that Read, his favorite broker, had returned to ICAP, coming out of retirement after less than a year so he could start earning again.

Still raw from the three years of internecine warfare between UBS's cash and trading desks that had expedited his departure, Hayes was keen not to repeat history. Citigroup arranged for a newly graduated swaps trader in his mid-twenties named Hayato Hoshino to relocate from Tokyo to the British capital. He would be Hayes's point of contact with the Citigroup cash desk, passing on requests to the bank's Libor submitters. Hoshino, oblivious to Hayes's plans, saw the move as a promotion and was delighted.[2]

Being able to influence Libor was only part of the solution to the puzzle. Cecere also set in motion plans for Citigroup to join the Tibor panel, which, Hayes would crow, was even easier to influence than Libor because fewer banks contributed to it. Hayes wanted to hit the ground running when he started trading, and being able to influence the two benchmarks that helped determine the profitability of the bulk of his positions was an important step. Another was bringing Citigroup's own London-based Libor-setters on board.

On the afternoon of Dec. 8, Cecere was at his desk on the Tokyo trading floor. He had an office but seldom used it, preferring to be amid the action. Cecere, who had his own trading book, believed that six-month yen Libor was too high. After checking the submissions from the previous day, he was surprised to see that Citigroup had input one of the highest figures.

Cecere contacted the head of the risk treasury team in Tokyo, Stantley Tan, and asked him to find out who the yen-setter was and request that he lower his input by several basis points. Risk treasury was the part of the bank responsible for borrowing and lending cash in different currencies to make sure the firm could meet its complex and ever-changing commitments. The division had teams around the world. The desk in Canary Wharf was responsible for the bank's Libor submissions.

"I spoke to Burak Celtik our point man in London," Tan wrote back to Cecere that afternoon, referring to the Turkish cash specialist who set the yen rates. "We agreed to coordinate more formally next year when Citigroup starts to quote Tibors. In the meantime I have asked him to consider moving quotes" lower.[3]

Cecere checked the Libors again later that night and was annoyed to see that Citigroup had only reduced its six-month rate by a quarter of a basis point.

"He's more than 2 [basis points] or up to 3 off market," Cecere wrote. "Can you speak with him again?"

The following day, Tan went back to the treasury desk in London as requested. "Was wondering if you could consider moving all quotes to lower end of quoted ranges as the yen money cash markets in practical terms are substantially lower," he wrote, pointing out that the bank's Libors were high relative to the bids they were seeing in Japan, where the majority of yen trading took place.

Tan forwarded the message chain to Andrew Thursfield, Citigroup's head of risk treasury in London. The response he got back from his U.K. counterpart left little room for misinterpretation: It was a thinly veiled warning to back off.

"The rules surrounding rate setting are strict," Thursfield wrote. "The contribution does have to be formed independently by the trader/desk in London who is responsible for the cash book based on the perceived London market offer. While additional information on relevant market activity can help as an input into the process, any recommendations or suggestions as to where rates should be set have to be disregarded."

Hayes, who sat just behind his boss, was not on the e-mail chain, but Cecere sent it to him.[4]

Thursfield was a straitlaced Englishman in his forties who had spent more than 20 years in risk management at Citigroup after joining as a graduate trainee. With rimless spectacles, a high-pitched, reedy voice and a deliberate way of speaking, he was more like an accountant than a banker. Thursfield saw himself as the guardian of the firm's balance sheet and didn't take kindly to being told how to do his job by a pushy American trader who knew nothing of the intricacies of bank funding.

Rather than lowering the inputs, Thursfield's team increased its submission days later, pushing the published Libor rates higher. Hayes would have to try a different tack. On Dec. 14 he sent an e-mail to Hoshino asking him to approach the rate-setters directly.

"Do you talk to the cash desk and did we know in advance?" Hayes asked, referring to the bank's decision to bump up its Libor submissions. "We need good dialogue with the cash desk. They can be invaluable to us. If we know ahead of time we can position and scalp the market."

The intransigence of the London rate-setters and Hoshino's lack of progress in striking up a rapport with them was frustrating for the derivatives traders in Tokyo, who, Hayes would later recall, often congregated in country head Brian McCappin's office.[5]

Hayes was scheduled to start trading in February 2010, once he'd prepared his systems and gone through his induction. Anxious to have everything in place before then, he flew to the U.K. in January to introduce Hoshino to the submitters and sweet-talk them into doing his bidding.

During his visit, Hayes took rate-setter Celtik, his manager Laurence Porter and Hoshino to lunch at Roka, an expensive, minimalist Japanese restaurant a few minutes' walk from Citigroup's Canary Wharf offices. Famous for its four-liter jars of shochu, a distilled Japanese drink that can be personalized for diners to enjoy on each visit for a cost of £280, Roka was popular with the bankers who plied their trade in the skyscrapers that surrounded the restaurant. It was a far cry from the fast-food joints that Hayes preferred, but he was there to impress.

Before the starters had arrived, Porter, a plainspoken Englishman with a deadpan demeanor who had been at Citigroup more than two decades, shut Hayes down. In words that echoed Thursfield's admonishment weeks earlier, he told Hayes that neither he nor Celtik could take into account his or any other trader's positions when making their submissions. Sharing market color—the nuggets of information that routinely pass between traders—was fine, but that was it, Porter said. Celtik remained quiet. There was no bespoke shochu drunk that day. The men were back at their desks within an hour and a quarter.[6]

What Hayes didn't realize was that no amount of schmoozing was going to get the rate-setters onside. Unlike some banks, Citigroup was taking the CFTC's investigation into Libor seriously. In March 2009, Thursfield had personally delivered an 18-page presentation via video-link to investigators on the rate-setting process. The cash traders weren't about to risk their necks for someone they didn't know who worked on the other side of the world in a different business area.

It wasn't just that they knew they were being watched. Thursfield was a stickler for the rules. A year earlier he'd joined the BBA's FXMMC, the body that oversaw the benchmark. While many of the committee's members weren't overly interested in the sanctity of the rate, Thursfield was. When the BBA issued fresh guidance on the rate-setting process, he sat down with his team individually and walked them through it.

Even if Thursfield wasn't so punctilious, there's no way he would have tried to accommodate Hayes. The pair had met three months earlier and Hayes had made a disastrous first impression. It was October 2009, shortly after Hayes had accepted the job at Citigroup, and Cecere had sent his new hire to London to meet the great and good.

"Good to meet you. You can help us out with Libors. I will let you know my axes," Hayes said by way of an opening gambit when he was introduced to Thursfield.[7]

Unshaven and disheveled, he told the Citigroup manager how the cash desk at UBS skewed its submissions to suit his book. He boasted of his close relationships with rate-setters at other banks and how they would do favors for each other. Hayes was trying to charm Thursfield, but he'd badly misjudged the man and the situation, and Thursfield took an instant dislike to him. The following day Thursfield got on the phone with his manager, Steve Compton, and relayed his concerns.

"Once you stray onto talking about Libor fixings, I mean we just paid another $75,000 bill to the lawyer this week for the work they're doing on the CFTC investigation," Thursfield said. "Whoever is the desk head, or whatever, [should] have a close watch on just what he's actually doing and how publicly. It's all, you know, very much barrow boy type" behavior—a derogatory British term derived from the lower-class youths who used to hawk fruit and vegetables from a wheelbarrow.

Hayes had also met Porter that day and made a similarly poor impression. When Thursfield asked him what he'd thought of Hayes, Porter told his boss he didn't think the bank should hire him.

It wasn't that Citigroup was a bastion of virtue. Over the previous decade the 200-year-old firm had been fined billions of dollars by regulators around the world for its involvement in scandals including the collapse of Enron and helping WorldCom defraud investors. In Japan the bank was seen as a black sheep by the local regulator. After Citigroup was stripped of its private-banking license there in 2004 for aggressive sales techniques and failing to curb money laundering, then-CEO Chuck Prince took a carefully choreographed seven-second bow at a press conference to demonstrate his contrition.[8] But in Thursfield, Hayes had come up against an immovable barrier.[9]

On returning to Tokyo after his lunch with the yen Libor-setters, Hayes was cautiously optimistic they would help him. As ever, his social radar was badly malfunctioning. He told Read at ICAP a few days later that he had got on well with Porter and that, while he probably couldn't be as open with his requests as he'd been at UBS, the Citigroup veteran was a man he could deal with—not some posh knob like a lot of the people in the industry.[10] Hayes had a tendency to hear what he wanted. In his mind, everything was falling into place as he intended.

After a few weeks getting prepared and snoozing through compulsory compliance classes, Hayes was ready to start trading again. Pumped full of adrenaline on his first day, he pulled the lines of four of his brokers in quick succession, astounding and horrifying his new colleagues. By the afternoon he'd run out of brokers and had to call one of them back and apologize just so he could place a trade. He dropped him again later that day.[11]

Since leaving UBS, Hayes had stayed in regular contact with the brokers and traders in his network, and on the afternoon of March 3, 2010, he was ready to bring them back into service. Just after 8 a.m. in London, Hayes picked up the phone and called Terry Farr.

"I have fixings for the first time today," Hayes said, getting straight to the point. "I need low 3s. HSBC is at 26 mate so he can come down a couple of points in 3s to 24."

Hayes knew that HSBC was one of the easiest banks to target. Farr had befriended the bank's latest rate-setter, Luke Madden, and regularly took him out for nights on the town. The bank wasn't a major player in the yen derivatives market, and Madden, who was never charged with a crime, was in the habit of calling up his pal Tel for guidance on where cash was trading before submitting his daily Libors.[12]

"I could try, mate, definitely," Farr replied haltingly. Something in his tone had changed. "I mean, with HSBC I asked him a little while ago and he fucking said to me not to ask him again but I will try, mate. They've all got right fucking funny on it recently."

Farr's response was a shock. The high-spirited RP Martin broker had always carried out Hayes's instructions without complaining. He wasn't the only bearer of bad news. Read also told Hayes that the rate-setters on the yen Libor panel were no longer paying much attention to Colin Goodman's daily run-through. Read would later say in court that, in reality, they never had.

It wasn't necessarily that Hayes's two most trusted brokers were unwilling to help him out, but rather that conditions had fundamentally changed. Banks were awash with cheap central bank money, interest rates were back at close to zero, and the cash markets were stable. The turmoil that had been such a feature of the market since the onset of the banking crisis in 2007 had dissipated. The rate-setters no longer needed Goodman or Farr to tell them where cash was trading since yen Libor barely moved at all anymore.

News of the CFTC's investigation was also starting to filter down, making everybody nervous. Even Adolph, the Deutsche Bank trader who'd been so helpful in the past, would soon start rebuffing him. When

Hayes asked for assistance, the Frenchman wrote back bluntly: "I have no influence or control, nor I want to be involved."[13]

Just after 4 p.m. in Tokyo, as his colleagues started to head home for the evening, Hayes stayed on at his desk determined to find a way to get the three-month rate lower. As he always liked to say, it was a numbers game. He typed out a message to Brent Davies, a former colleague at RBS in London and one of his few real friends in the market. After more than a decade at RBS, Davies, who had flowing locks down to his shoulders, had switched careers and become a broker at ICAP in London. He was still tight with Paul White, the rate-setter at RBS, and, Hayes figured, he might be able to pull in a favor.

"I really need a low 3M yen Libor," Hayes wrote. "Even if he only moves 3M down 1 basis point from 25 to 24."

"I'll give him a nudge later, see what we can do," said Davies, who has never been charged. "Haven't seen him since I left so might buy him a steak to catch up." White, a long-standing but relatively junior employee at RBS, was well known for liking his food.

Next, Hayes turned his attention to Hoshino in London. The strait-laced yen rate-setter Celtik was on vacation that week, so Hayes suggested Hoshino try his boss Porter.

"If they could move 3M lower by 1 basis point for a few weeks, it would help," Hayes said. "Make sure not to put it in writing. Just have a quiet word with him."

The next day, RBS's three-month yen rate fell by 1 basis point. Citigroup also lowered its submission by half a basis point. At last, Citigroup's in-house setters were helping him, Hayes thought. In fact it was probably just a coincidence—there's no evidence Hoshino even passed on the message.[14] Still, that day's published rate fell 0.2 of a basis point, a decent result under the circumstances.

Hayes wasn't overly concerned about the lack of volatility or what his brokers were telling him about their waning influence, as long as he was still making money. And in his first few months of trading in 2010 he was up about $50 million.[15]

That all changed in early May when, saddled with debt and mired in corruption, Greece took a 110 billion-euro bailout from the International Monetary Fund, the European Commission and the European Central Bank (ECB). It was during Golden Week, a national holiday in Japan, and Hayes was supposed to be enjoying the break with Sarah. Instead he spent the whole time glued to his BlackBerry while his positions whipsawed by $10 million to $15 million a day.

Hayes had put on a big trade betting, correctly, that Europe's nascent sovereign-debt crisis would worsen and that the cost of borrowing euros for longer periods would shoot higher relative to overnight rates as banks stockpiled their cash. He'd hedged his position in the dollar market but hadn't anticipated that borrowing costs in dollars would shoot up even more as investors scrambled for the safe haven of the U.S. currency. That miscalculation was costing him dearly. In the weeks that followed, he lost $80 million and Citigroup forced him to cut some of his positions.

By early June, Hayes's gift for making enemies was also hurting him. After a Citigroup colleague quit and joined Deutsche Bank, he leaked details of Hayes's trading positions, including, Hayes believed, to Pieri. He was now playing with his cards exposed. He felt betrayed by the UBS manager he'd looked up to like a father.[16]

At the tail end of one of the worst months in his trading career, with his losses mounting by the day and his old allies deserting him, Hayes was getting desperate. He'd only been at the bank six months and was already in a dire predicament. On June 25, he picked up his phone and dialed Hoshino's mobile number.

Hoshino had told Hayes repeatedly over the past few weeks that the rate setters weren't happy talking about Libor. In reality, the young trader, who'd earned the nickname "Little Hoshino", never really tried. On several occasions the shy, slight newcomer had walked over to the risk treasury desk, hung around for a few minutes like a ghost, then trundled back to his seat again without saying a word. The cash traders were utterly perplexed.[17]

This time Hayes wasn't going to take no for an answer. He ordered Hoshino to approach Celtik and ask for a high six-month submission going into the end of the month. A few days earlier he'd coached him to catch the rate-setter on his way to the toilet so their colleagues wouldn't overhear them.

Hoshino made the short walk across the trading floor to Celtik's desk and asked, as politely as he could, whether he would mind inputting a high six-month rate as a favor for his boss. It was a fatal misstep. The CFTC had just written to Citigroup and 15 other banks and ordered them to carry out an internal probe into whether their traders were trying to rig the rate.

Only too aware of the regulatory heat, Celtik told Hoshino what had been drummed into him by his bosses: It would not be appropriate for him to take into account a derivatives trader's positions when making a submission. After Hoshino left, Celtik swiveled in his chair and relayed what had happened to Porter, who told him to report it to Thursfield immediately. Some people may have dealt with the matter discreetly, reaching out to Hayes's boss and warning him to keep the trader in check. Thursfield followed protocol to the letter, notifying senior managers and alerting compliance. Citigroup's hotshot new trader in Japan was now on the radar.

Hayes had no idea what had just happened in London or the repercussions it would have. As ever, his mind was squarely on his trading book, and he was stressed. Waking on Saturday, Hayes composed an e-mail to Cecere and Morton apologizing for how much money he'd lost and promising to make amends. Morton told him not to worry, but said that he needed to reduce his risk—the size of the bets he had outstanding—as soon as possible. It was a blow to Hayes's ego.

While Hayes was unwinding his positions in Tokyo in the weeks that followed, Citigroup's lawyers and compliance officers in London were poring over every e-mail, instant message and recorded phone call he'd made since arriving at the bank. Hoshino was pulled in for questioning, as were Celtik and some of the other rate-setters.

Cecere got wind of the situation on July 12. He waited until the Japanese markets had closed and called Morton, the one man at the bank who he knew would give it to him straight.

"I have a question for you: is there some issue with Little Hoshino in London and risk treasury? Did those guys, like, report him?" Cecere said.

"They feel like they, you know, multiple times, uh, you know, um, sort of pushed back," Morton told him. "Thursfield is being subpoenaed by the SEC, you know, so they figure 'fuck, if we have people visit us like this and, you know, we should log it with compliance.'"

Cecere couldn't believe what he was hearing. "Those fucking cunts," he spat. "What is wrong with them? Pardon my language, but that drives me fucking mental. Pick up a phone and have a word with me."

"I've told you, dude, multiple times, be fucking careful with those guys," Morton replied.

"What the fuck kind of bank is this?" said Cecere. "Turn your people in instead of just picking up a phone and saying: 'look this is really not comfortable, please drop it.'"

Hayes didn't hear about the internal investigation until later that month. Cecere rang him on his mobile on a Sunday and suggested they go for a drink. They met that evening at the Windsor Bar, a U.K.-themed pub in Tokyo where the American was a regular, Hayes would later testify. Over a beer and a Coca-Cola, Cecere told Hayes that he was going to be questioned by Citigroup's lawyers that week as part of a probe into Libor.

Over the next few weeks, Hayes spent more than 12 hours being quizzed by Citigroup's in-house and external lawyers. He stuck firmly to the same line: That he had no idea what Hoshino had said to the London rate-setters or why. Hayes assumed he was being questioned as part of a wider investigation, but strange things started happening that made him nervous. Attachments to e-mails he was trying to send kept getting blocked, and he was prevented from leaving the office one evening with some documents. What annoyed Hayes more than anything else was that the lawyers kept pulling him off the desk during trading hours, which was costing him money.

Increasingly frantic, he sent Cecere an e-mail at the end of August asking whether he was being singled out by the probe. He didn't get a reply.

A week later, as Hayes strode across the trading floor to his desk, he got a tap on the shoulder and was pulled into a meeting room. It was a Monday morning. As he walked in, he would later recall, he saw Morton and McCappin, the CEO for Japan, sitting at a conference table. He hadn't even known that Morton was in town. Citigroup's local head of HR, Moira Lynam, was also there, as was Akiko Yamahara, the bank's general counsel in the country.

Hayes was told that the bank had been investigating him for weeks and had uncovered multiple instances of him trying to manipulate yen Libor to benefit his trading positions. Not only had he been attempting to influence the bank's own rate-setters but he had been acting in concert with traders at other banks and interdealer brokers. Such conduct

violated the bank's code of conduct, and probably the law, and conse-
quently he was being fired immediately.

Hayes was floored. Every time he'd asked his bosses what was going
on they'd told him not to worry.[18] The previous week he'd been trading
as usual. Recovering quickly from the shock, Hayes came out swinging.

"Well that's sort of ironic that you're firing me given that you
were involved in it up to your eyeballs as well," he later recalled telling
McCappin, who eyed him from across the table. [19]

"Oh, but he wasn't, he didn't have any trading positions," Yamahara
interjected.

"That's not really true is it?" Hayes shot back at McCappin. "As a
CEO you have responsibility for every trading position the bank's got.
How much are you going to pay me to go quietly? Otherwise I'm going
to make a real fuss about this."

All eyes were trained on Hayes. They'd heard about his vitriol on the
trading floor. Now it was directed at them. Ever the trader, Hayes knew
the strength of his position. When he stopped ranting, they asked him to
leave the room.

A few minutes later Hayes was called back. This time he was told
that, while he wouldn't be getting any more money, he could keep his
$3 million signing bonus. In Hayes's eyes it was hush money.[20] There was
nothing more to be said.

Chapter 14

Just Keep Swimming

Just before her 16th birthday in 1501, an auburn-haired Spanish princess set sail for England, where she was betrothed to marry the king's eldest son. The journey ended on a grand country estate set within the rolling hills of Hampshire, where she met for the first time Arthur and his rather more strapping younger brother Henry. Within a year her young husband was dead, struck down by sweating sickness, and Henry VIII and Catherine of Aragon were engaged to be married.

On the same grounds, dressed in a morning suit, navy tie and cream waistcoat, his blond hair uncharacteristically neat, Tom Hayes stood smiling for the cameras, one hand clasping a half full glass of champagne, the other on the small of his wife's back. Hayes and Tighe were married in a lavish ceremony on a September Saturday in 2010, less than two weeks after Hayes was fired. The venue was the Four Seasons Hotel Hampshire, an elegantly restored 130-room Georgian manor house a short drive from the village where Tighe's family lived. After the vows, guests congregated on the estate's manicured lawns and watched the sun descend, casting a dappled light on a lake in the middle distance. Among them were Hayes's broker Noel Cryan and former RBS colleague Brent Davies. In the evening, a spectacular fireworks display lit up the night sky.

Hayes appeared happy and relaxed, but the last few days had been brutal. Three days after his dismissal, he'd handed Citigroup a letter Sarah had helped him draft. "I refute that my actions constituted any wrongdoing and further to our discussion in the meeting held on Sept. 6, 2010, I wish to reiterate that my actions were entirely consistent with those of others at senior levels in Citigroup Global Markets Japan," Hayes wrote to the bank's HR department. "Furthermore, and as I have previously stated, the senior management at CGMJ were aware of my actions and at no point was I told that my actions could or would constitute any wrongdoing."[1]

Hayes claimed that his attempts to influence benchmark interest rates had been condoned and supported by his manager Cecere, who would also soon be pushed out of the bank, as well as Morton and Tokyo boss McCappin.

The couple briefly returned to Tokyo after the wedding, but by now they were ready to come back to England for good. They paid £1 million cash for a luxury penthouse apartment in East London and looked forward to a fresh start. Before long, Sarah discovered she was pregnant. Hayes perused brochures for MBA programs. Then, one afternoon at the end of March, Hayes received an unexpected phone call from his junior at UBS, Mirhat Alykulov.

Hayes and Alykulov had a productive, albeit fractious relationship during their three years together at UBS. The pair sat next to each other, and Hayes had acted as a mentor of sorts to the compact Kazakh trader affectionately known as Meerkat. Together they helped the yen desk's revenues skyrocket. Alykulov was a fitness nut who would later compete in amateur boxing matches under the moniker "the angry teddy bear". At work he was a relaxed, jovial character, and over time he learned not to take it personally when Hayes berated him. If things got too serious he lightened the mood with Borat impressions. When Hayes was on holiday, Alykulov passed on the desk's Libor requests to the brokers. After Hayes joined Citigroup, Alykulov was promoted and the pair remained on friendly terms.

That ended abruptly when Hayes was fired. News of his dismissal spread through the market on instant-message chats and mobile-phone screens like a virus. Hayes had become a pariah. Alykulov ignored his former colleague's efforts to contact him via social media and on iPhone's FaceTime video-call service. At one point he removed Hayes from his Facebook friends list, prompting Hayes to send him a message asking why, accompanied by a sad-face emoticon.

Now, after months of radio silence, Alykulov was phoning Hayes for a chat. What Hayes didn't know was that Alykulov was making the call from an attorney's office in Washington on a line that was being monitored by the FBI. A few days earlier, Alykulov had been flown to the U.S. and driven to an airless interrogation room in the fraud section at the Justice Department, where two government agents took turns laying out the evidence against him: e-mails and chats of Alykulov asking traders and brokers to help move the rate. Hayes had taught his young disciple well. With the U.S.'s harsh sentencing regime for white-collar crime, Alykulov was looking at several years behind bars.

Then they offered him an alternative. If Alykulov told them every-thing, the agents said, they might be able to make this all go away. Faced with a lengthy jail term, he spilled his guts. After four exhausting days, the trader, still in his late twenties, was given his prize: an agreement from the Justice Department not to prosecute. Before he could fly back to Japan, they just needed him to do one last thing.

So it was that at around noon on March 29, 2011, Alykulov sat, receiver in hand, preparing to sink his old trading partner. Wiretaps and other covert surveillance techniques are rarely used in white-collar cases because news about criminal investigations tends to leak, alerting poten-tial targets to keep quiet. Libor was different. Few traders had been inter-viewed, and so far there had been little coverage in the media. It was too good an opportunity for the FBI to pass up. They set up an 800 number that would display on Hayes's screen as coming from Alykulov's Japan-registered cell phone but would in fact be linked to a recording device at the Justice Department's headquarters in Washington.

Alykulov perched on the edge of a chair in a conference room in his attorney's offices. The lawyer, who had agreed not to listen in on a second line in case Hayes heard him breathing, sat on the other side of the room poised with a pen and a notepad. Alykulov pushed the numbers slowly. After what seemed like an age, Hayes picked up.

"Hey, Tom," Alykulov said, as casually as he could manage. "I got your Facebook message. What's happening?" As ever, Hayes ignored the small talk and dived straight in. Has UBS said anything about speaking to the feds?

Alykulov, desperately trying to hold it together, told Hayes they were leaning on him to talk. One of the Justice Department's goals was to get

Hayes on record attempting to persuade Alykulov to lie to the authorities. Under U.S. law, if you know there's a government investigation going on and you try to obstruct it or cause it to be misled in some way, they can throw the book at you. Hayes paused, as if somehow aware of the trap that was lying in front of him.

"The U.S. Department of Justice, mate, you know, they're like…the dudes who, you know, you know, absolutely like, you know, you know….put people in jail," Hayes said. "Why the hell would you want to talk to them?"

Each time Alykulov brought up Libor or their time at UBS, Hayes went quiet and the conversation petered out. When Alykulov called Hayes a few days later and tried again, he was even less forthcoming. No matter. Alas, for Hayes, the authorities already had more than enough to build a case against him.

Back in 2008, UBS had hired Allen & Overy to help handle the CFTC's preliminary inquiry into Libor, which at that stage was focused on low-balling in the dollar rate. UBS and the British law firm found nothing remiss, and in the months that followed UBS shunned the authorities' entreaties for greater cooperation.[2] After Barclays came forward in 2010 with evidence that its traders were manipulating Libor for profit and the authorities ordered banks to carry out internal probes, UBS reopened its investigation into the dollar rates business. In the first week of December, it stumbled upon a hand grenade.

Buried among a dossier of so-called hot documents pulled together as part of the initial probe was the July 3, 2009, e-mail sent by Pieri to a group of senior UBS executives lobbying to secure a bigger bonus for Hayes, who was threatening to leave for Citigroup. The recipients of the e-mail, in which Pieri had listed among Hayes's attributes his "strong connections with Libor setters in London", included the head and the chairman of its investment bank.

On the same e-mail chain was the rebuttal sent by Darin, Hayes's antagonist at UBS, after his boss Yvan Ducrot asked him to provide some counter-arguments. Hayes does "know some of the traders at other banks from his London days", Darin wrote, "but personally I find it embarrassing when he calls up his mates to ask for favours on high/low fixings. It makes UBS appear to manipulate others to suit our position," and besides "what's the legal risk of UBS asking others to move their fixing?"[3]

It was a lucky break for the authorities. UBS's investigators had only landed upon the correspondence because it was sent to senior managers who were being examined as part of the probe into dollar Libor. At that stage nobody had considered looking into the yen operation. "Who the hell is Tom Hayes?" wondered UBS's Americas general counsel Mark Shelton, the baby-faced former Georgetown University professor running the internal investigation.

Shelton, who once served as counsel for Bob Dole's run at the presidency, ordered his team to pull Hayes's chats. They were filtered using key words like "low 6m" and "favour". After a nervous couple of days, Shelton was sitting in his office in New York when the phone calls began: "Hey, Mark, we've found something." Every 15 minutes Shelton would get another call, each one more distressing than the last. The picture that emerged was horrifying. From the first weeks of his probation in the summer of 2006 until he walked out the door in September 2009, Hayes and his colleagues had made more than 2,000 documented requests on at least 570 days.[4] The trader had sought to manipulate Libor about three-quarters of the times he was in the office and made almost no attempt to hide it.

A stunned Shelton called UBS's senior executives in Zurich, London and New York and laid out the situation. The bank was in a tough position. It was already the subject of criminal investigations into tax evasion and municipal bond fraud. The last thing it needed was to get embroiled in another scandal. On the other hand, there was no hiding from the mountains of evidence piling up in front of them.

For the UBS executives, the immediate question was: How the hell did we miss this?

Some blamed Allen & Overy for failing to dig out the incriminating e-mails and highlight their significance. It was, according to one senior lawyer representing the bank, a "colossal fuck up". Others say the firm had a limited role and reacted promptly once the issues with the yen business emerged. Either way, the two sides quietly agreed it would be best to part ways.[5]

In the end, the decision over what to do next was easy: UBS admitted everything and begged for forgiveness. In one day in December 2010, Shelton held back-to-back meetings in his office with representatives from various authorities. It was what's known in legal circles as a "come to Jesus" moment. Fear of reprisals wasn't the only motivating factor. The antitrust division of the Justice Department has a policy of granting leniency to the first member of a conspiracy to reach out and fess up. That means that, regardless of how much of a prominent role a corporation played in a cartel, it can escape censure by bringing it to the attention of the authorities. No fines, no guilty plea, no license revoked.

Eventually, UBS was granted a marker, meaning that as long as it continued to cooperate with the antitrust division, it would be given immunity from prosecution. The decision was controversial. The Justice Department's leniency provisions are designed to encourage corporations to come forward and blow the whistle on anti-competitive practices, but the CFTC had been investigating Libor, and UBS specifically, since 2008—albeit for lowballing the dollar rate rather than the profit-motivated actions of Hayes and his colleagues. Plus, it was Barclays, not UBS, that had been the first to come forward with evidence derivatives traders were rigging the rate, something the authorities had been completely in the dark about. For reasons known only to itself, the British bank had so far failed to seek antitrust leniency.

The sudden willingness of UBS to provide information opened a schism within the DOJ. Despite the shared crest, the attorneys in the antitrust and criminal divisions were in direct competition: for resources, for prestige, for the attention of the attorney general. Fraud, which sits in the criminal division, considered Libor its case and didn't take kindly to antitrust stealing its thunder. In the end, the two sides agreed on a compromise. UBS would be granted leniency for its antitrust infractions, and the fraud section would be free to pursue the bank over other criminal offenses such as wire fraud. Representatives from both sides would attend interviews with employees of the bank, although fraud would take the lead.

Shortly after securing its marker, UBS retained Gary Spratling, a partner at Gibson Dunn & Crutcher in Los Angeles. Spratling, a squat man with sleek, red-tinged hair and a moustache, was Mr. Antitrust. He'd spent 28 years at the antitrust division, including as its head, and was now so adept at getting clients out of scrapes they'd taken to calling him Spratman.[6] In the first months of 2011, his team embarked on a kind of regulatory world tour, taking in Japan, Canada, Belgium, Switzerland and the U.K. Anywhere UBS was exposed, Spratman and his lawyers visited to confess the bank's sins and seek leniency.[7]

Meanwhile, back in Washington, the motley and ever-growing coalition of criminal and civil authorities investigating Libor began to interview anyone connected with UBS's yen derivatives business. Traders who sat near Hayes in Tokyo, managers who had nurtured and protected him, low-ranking rate-setters in Zurich—all were grilled in bank offices and interrogation rooms around the world. When they were through with them, the authorities moved on to the traders and brokers Hayes had colluded with at other firms. Interviewees sat at one end of a large, square conference table, flanked by at least two of their own lawyers. To their left were members of the CFTC, who sat next to people from the FCA, who were alongside the folks from the fraud section, who were flanked by representatives from antitrust. Junior attorneys stood against the walls and took notes. Even the SEC, keen to get in on the action, sent a handful of people. For some interviews there were as many as 40 people in the room, all with their eyes on a lone trader, often a long way from home. The interviews were conducted by investigators from the FBI, expert interrogators who'd cut their teeth breaking Mafia bosses and terrorists. The traders didn't stand a chance.

■ ■ ■

It's not clear how much Hayes knew about what was going on in Washington.

The authorities never questioned him—they had so much evidence they didn't need to—and few of his old friends in the market were willing to reach out to keep him in the loop. But there were worrying portents. From the fall of 2011, some of Hayes's contacts were suspended from their firms. At RBS, Neil Danziger, the forwards trader who had taken the other side of Hayes's wash trades, was pushed out the door. So was Paul White, the low-ranking rate-setter who'd accommodated Hayes's requests for the promise of a steak dinner. Around the same time at Deutsche Bank, Guillaume Adolph was suspended, along with colleagues.[8] And Alykulov and Pieri were also reportedly out of the market.

Then, on Dec. 16, 2011, more than a year after Hayes had left, the Japanese Financial Services Agency issued a notice banning Citigroup from trading derivatives tied to yen Libor and Tibor for two weeks. The release was covered in the media, and for the first time Libor rigging by traders started to become a news story. Fortunately for Hayes, the Japanese regulator stopped short of naming him and Cecere. It would be a while before the mysterious Trader A would be outed in the press.

As the tide rose around them, Hayes and his wife built themselves a fortress. In December, shortly after the birth of their son Joshua, the couple moved into the Old Rectory, a six-bedroom property in Woldingham, a pretty village in Surrey with its own cricket club, private boarding school and Anglican church. The 4,000-square-foot property is set on the corner of a large, well-kept private road with views over the hills and meadows of the North Downs. They paid the £1.2 million asking price in cash.[9]

Woldingham could be any other idyllic English village, except that it is less than 20 miles south of the City of London. That combination makes it one of the richest suburbs in the country, and an ideal base for stockbrokers and company executives.[10] Houses with names like Little Oaks and The Hermitage are concealed behind long driveways and guarded by gates with electronic intercoms. Past residents enticed by its friendly seclusion include a former head of the British secret service, H.G. Wells's mistress and, more recently, glamor model-turned-author Katie Price. No matter how famous, all residents are encouraged to participate in village life. In the winter, the focus is the pantomime held at the village hall. The year the Hayeses arrived it was *Peter Pan*.

While Sarah integrated herself into village life, Hayes was more preoccupied. Just because he wasn't working for a bank, didn't mean he had to stop trading. Hayes put about £1 million of his money from Citigroup into an online brokerage account, which he used to bet on currencies and stock indexes. Before long he had almost doubled it.[11]

When he wasn't at his computer, Hayes embarked on a project to expand and refurbish the Old Rectory. In February 2012, plans were filed for a three-story extension, adding a new wing with a large seventh bedroom. After that application was approved, he submitted a proposal to erect a six-foot electric gate to keep out intruders. Inside, the kitchen was overhauled using granite surfaces and hi-tech appliances. Bathrooms covered in Italian marble and limestone were added to every bedroom. Japanese artwork was hung on the walls to complement the pinewood floorboards and handmade furniture.[12]

With time on his hands, Hayes also learned to drive. He astounded a friend by memorizing the entire 168-page Highway Code and bought a Mercedes CLK.[13]

Hayes began a one-year MBA program at the London branch of Hult Business School. Students were divided into small groups for classes testing soft skills like networking and building relationships. After spending his twenties as a cutthroat, every-man-for-himself trader, Hayes was reinventing himself as a team player. Each morning he drove to Hult's campus in central London from the flat they were staying in while the renovations were going on. His classmates were an international group of budding entrepreneurs, technologists and managers. The hotshot trader was something of a novelty, revered by the boys who dreamed of making it big in global finance. One former classmate recalls watching Hayes trading currencies on his mobile phone during class. When he asked him how much he'd just made, Hayes casually replied "£17,000".

At first Hayes came across as standoffish, but slowly he came out of his shell, joining his classmates after lectures for cheap pints and games of pool. He thrived, making new friends and impressing his tutors. On one occasion, a professor gave Hayes' group more than 90 percent for a corporate finance assignment, docking a couple of points for getting some sums wrong. Hayes was adamant they were correct and spent the class checking and rechecking his math. When the lesson was over he walked over to his tutor and demanded she look again. He was right, and the group's marks were increased.

Life passed by in a haze of new beginnings. When his classmates asked about his former life, he told them about days spent flying first class between offices. Few knew why he had left the industry. If a friend did ask how he was coping, he repeated a mantra from the Disney movie *Finding Nemo* about a small fish that finds itself among sharks in unfamiliar waters: "Just keep swimming".

As the course came to an end in the summer of 2012, Hayes and one of his classmates, a larger-than-life American with a mane of blonde ringlets named Jennifer Arcuri, hatched a plan to start their own business. They were an odd couple. Arcuri was at the center of student life at Hult, a vivacious socializer who would go on to set up her own tech startup networking company. The business she launched with Hayes, Title X Technology, sold software and marketing solutions carried out by low-cost developers in Bulgaria. It was incorporated in July 2012, a month after they graduated.

A few weeks later, Hayes stood beaming in a green and white felt dinosaur costume, his arm draped around a Frenchman in a beret and a striped sweater. It was Halloween 2012 and Arcuri, dressed as a Bavarian barmaid, had organized a party for her friends and the recent Hult graduates at a bar in Shoreditch. At one stage, the crowd parted to watch Jesus thrash Dracula in a breakdancing competition. As the evening unfolded, a bright, new generation of bleary-eyed entrepreneurs toasted shot glasses and looked forward to a future that was theirs for the taking.

Chapter 15

The Ballad of Diamond Bob

On June 27, 2012—four years, two months and 11 days after *The Wall Street Journal* raised the alarm—Barclays became the first bank to reach a settlement with the authorities for rigging Libor. At 2 p.m. in London, 9 a.m. in Washington, the CFTC, the Justice Department and the FSA simultaneously pushed out notices outlining the bank's transgressions and issuing fines totaling $453 million.

The offenses outlined in the documents fell into two categories: Traders, principally in New York, had, between 2005 and 2009, pressured the individuals responsible for submitting Libor in London to alter their inputs to suit their derivatives positions; and managers, mostly in London, had ordered rate-setters to lowball their figures during the crisis.

Just as striking as what the bank's employees did was the brazen way they talked about it. Investigators cherry picked the most shocking e-mails and instant messages for maximum impact. They were gift wrapped for journalists.

In one chat, a former Barclays trader who had moved to another firm thanked a current employee who'd helped him influence that day's rate by typing: "Dude. I owe you big time! Come over one day after work and I'm opening a bottle of Bollinger."[1] In another, a trader asked a rate-setter: "If it's not too late low 1m and 3m would be nice, but please feel free to say no," to which the submitter replied: "Done…for you big boy."

Nobody at Barclays expected to get an easy ride, but the mood at the bank's headquarters in Canary Wharf that summer afternoon was surprisingly upbeat. In a conference room adjoining the trading floor shortly before the announcement, salesmen and women, the shiny folk who interact with clients, were told to brace themselves for turbulence. Don't talk to anyone, even your family, their managers said, and it will all blow over by the weekend.

That sense of optimism stemmed from the top of the organization. Despite the reprimands and record fines, Barclays's senior managers and lawyers felt they had made the best of a bad situation. Their willingness to go to the authorities first was acknowledged in unprecedented terms in the notices. The Justice Department cited Barclays's "extraordinary cooperation" and pointed out that the bank had volunteered fresh information that was not known to them. As a result, the fines were much lower than they would have been, and a fraction of those later levied on other firms.[2]

More importantly, Barclays's lawyers at Sullivan & Cromwell had negotiated a non-prosecution agreement with the U.S. government, the best possible outcome for a corporation found culpable in a criminal investigation. In exchange for Barclays paying a fine and agreeing to overhaul the way it set and scrutinized Libor, the Justice Department agreed not to press charges. It was a major coup. When UBS settled a few months later, it was forced to cop a guilty plea at its Japanese subsidiary. Deutsche Bank's U.K. unit also pleaded guilty, while Rabobank was given a two-year deferred-prosecution agreement, something akin to a suspended sentence.[3]

Shortly before the Barclays notices were published, the bank issued its own statement announcing that Bob Diamond would be foregoing his year-end bonus, along with senior managers Rich Ricci and Jerry Del Missier and Finance Director Chris Lucas. The overriding sense in the executive suite was that Barclays was the good guy and would be recognized as such when the dust settled. The advantages of being the first mover had been drummed into the bank's executives from the moment they first came forward with evidence more than two years earlier. For a short while it looked as if it might have been the right decision. Barclays shares closed 2 percent higher that day.

Meanwhile, over at Mackey's Public House in Washington the CFTC investigators were having a blast. After a grueling day dealing with other agencies and giving press interviews, Gensler and his team crammed into the dingy Irish pub two blocks from their office and celebrated with beer and nachos.[4] It was a big moment in the history of the agency and the highlight of many of the investigators' careers. For Gensler it was particularly poignant: It was the anniversary of his wife Francesca's death. The little-agency-that-could had arrived.

All the main players were there: McGonagle, the manager who'd kick-started the investigation in 2008; Lowe and Termine, the tag team that had driven it home. Other folk joined them later in the evening, when the barman cranked up the Irish music and the clientele grew boisterous and misty-eyed.

One man was conspicuous by his absence. Obie, the acting head of enforcement who had played such a key part in getting the investigation off the ground, had been taken off the case at the end of 2010 and sent back to New York after he wasn't given the role permanently. In his place was a polished, triathlon-running Skadden Arps partner named David Meister.

Meister, a former assistant U.S. attorney at the Southern District of New York, had the swagger Gensler told confidants he wanted at the agency, with its new responsibilities and heightened profile. On his first day, Gensler told him one of his main tasks was getting Libor over the line. It hadn't been an easy ride.

Even after UBS and Barclays came forward, there had been roadblocks. Traders refused to cooperate with the investigation or maintained that it was all a misunderstanding; banks including Deutsche Bank missed deadlines and lost crucial documents; and the agency wasted months attempting to quantify losses from individual bank's actions—an essential step if it wanted to force them to pay restitution to victims—before concluding that it couldn't be done.[5]

Then, at the end of 2011, just as the authorities were preparing to wrap up the Barclays probe, a new body was found in the undergrowth. Banks came forward with evidence that suggested a clique of high-flying traders at several firms had also worked together to rig Euribor, the benchmark for euros administered by the European Banking Federation in Brussels. It was an audacious feat: With more than 40 banks submitting rates each day, Euribor was mathematically much harder to rig than Libor. The discovery pushed the investigation back by months.

The deeper the investigators dug, the more evidence of manipulation they found. Obscure new benchmarks were discovered that shared the same vulnerabilities as Libor. Padded envelopes containing CDs of fresh evidence arrived every other day, eliciting sighs from the already overworked individuals on the cases. Soon, the list of firms implicated was in double figures. More than 200 traders and brokers from around the world were caught up in the scam, affecting interest rates in at least half a dozen currencies.

By the spring of 2012, Gensler's patience had run out. The CFTC carries out about 500 investigations a year, mostly into small-scale misdemeanors like registration violations and tin-pot Ponzi schemes. Each time an investigation is wrapped up the agency's five commissioners sign off before it's announced to the public. In a heated meeting, Gensler told Meister no further enforcement actions would pass through his office until the Barclays settlement was out. Case files described as hostages were held for weeks in a cardboard container that ominously came to be known as "the Box".

When the Barclays settlement was published, the hostages were finally released.

Gensler signed the box and left it on Meister's desk as a souvenir, and as the beer flowed at Mackey's that night any animosity that had built up between the two men washed away on a tide of bonhomie.

■ ■ ■

The next morning, confidence at Barclays headquarters in London was wavering. Newspaper editors and politicians largely ignored the fact that Barclays had been the first to come forward. All they saw was that traders at the bank had been joyfully rigging the world's most important number for years. Diamond's decision to forego his multimillion-pound bonus seemed like a woefully inadequate response to such flagrant greed and corruption. The narrative had begun to shift uncomfortably toward the flashy American at the top of the firm.

"If Bob Diamond had a scintilla of shame, he would resign," Matthew Oakeshott, a Liberal Democrat peer, said in an interview with the influential morning radio program *Today*, expressing a widely shared view. "If Barclays's board had an inch of backbone between them, they would sack him."

When Prime Minister David Cameron weighed in and told reporters the Barclays management team had "serious questions to answer", the markets sat up and took notice. By midday, the shares had tumbled 10 percent.

What Barclays and its lawyers had failed to factor in to their considerations was that Diamond had a target on his back.[6] Incredibly, nobody at the bank had ever thought to consult any public relations professionals.[7] In 2010, with the crisis fresh in people's memories, Diamond had taken home a reported £63 million in compensation and awards, leading then-Business Secretary Peter Mandelson to describe him as "the unacceptable face of banking".[8] Eight months later, he'd sparked a fresh round of headlines when he told a group of MPs assembled to quiz him ahead of his elevation to the role of group CEO: "There was a period of remorse and apology…that period needs to be over."[9]

Bonuses for the deeply competitive Diamond were always more about keeping score with his rivals than the money, says a former board member. He strived to be on a par with the biggest names on Wall Street like JPMorgan's Jamie Dimon and Goldman Sachs's Lloyd Blankfein, and he genuinely couldn't understand the objections.

It wasn't just Diamond's lack of contrition that stuck in the craw. British authorities were growing increasingly frustrated at Barclays's habit of pushing the bounds of acceptability in its interpretation of regulations. Correspondence between Barclays Chairman Marcus Agius and the FSA published in the aftermath of the settlement reveal an increasingly antagonistic relationship between the bank and its main regulator.

The FSA's grievances, outlined in one April 2012 letter, were extensive: A controversial 2010 deal called Protium, which allowed Barclays to shift assets to the Cayman Islands to gain a preferable accounting treatment; the revelation in February 2011 that the bank had paid just £113 million, or 1 percent, in U.K. corporation tax on £11.6 billion of profit in 2009; the widespread misselling of Payment Protection Insurance to retail customers; the deliberate overvaluation of the assets on its balance sheet.[10]

All this took place during a period of festering hostility toward the banks. Following in the footsteps of demonstrators around the world, 3,000 angry protesters had taken to the streets on Oct. 15, 2011, to seize the London Stock Exchange. When they were turned away, they made their way to St. Paul's Cathedral and set up camp. For months, the white stone steps of the iconic London landmark were littered with tents full of activists rallying against the growing chasm between the wealthiest 1 percent and the rest of society.

Earlier that summer, the U.K. had witnessed its worst rioting since the 1980s after a young, black man was shot and killed by police in North London. Violent protests spread across the country culminating in five deaths and £200 million of property damage. News bulletins were dominated for days by apocalyptic images of looting youths in hoodies against a backdrop of buildings blazing in the night sky.

The hoodies weren't the only ones feeling angry. Economic growth was stagnating around the world, accompanied by rising unemployment and cuts to welfare spending. Savings dwindled as equity markets struggled to bounce back. In Europe, the inability of Greece, Portugal and Spain to honor their rising debts threatened the stability of the entire region. To see bankers thriving in such circumstances seemed an affront. By the time the Libor settlement was published it was, in the words of one investigator, like throwing a match into an arid field. Barclays shares closed the day down 16 percent, the biggest drop in more than three years.

■ ■ ■

Marcus Agius joined Barclays in the bull market of 2006 after more than 30 years advising CEOs and government ministers at prestigious boutique investment bank Lazard. Discreet, unflappable and well connected, the trim, silver-haired son of an army lieutenant colonel was exactly the kind of a person one would want around in a crisis. By 6 p.m. on Friday, June 29, 2012, he was squarely in the middle of one.

Seated at the head of the large, hull-shaped conference table that dominates Barclays's 31st floor boardroom, the 65-year-old Englishman cast his eyes at the executives and advisers around him. As chairman, Agius had been one of a handful of individuals responsible for the decision to settle with regulators first. It was now glaringly obvious what a mistake that had been.

It had been another desperate day. That morning, in a fresh scandal, the U.K. financial regulator had issued a statement suggesting banks, including Barclays, had missold complex derivatives to thousands of unsuspecting small businesses. In newspaper articles, owners of fish-and-chip shops in the north of England complained of being saddled with debt after buying interest-rate swaps they didn't need or understand from pushy bankers in pinstriped suits.[11]

When the hubbub of conversation died down, Agius stood and, voice barely raised, explained why he'd called the emergency meeting. Barclays was in trouble. The hordes were baying on the streets outside, and they needed to do something to sate them. Diamond listened from across the table.

Lucas, the bank's CFO, spoke up first. Despite the hysteria, he told the room, we're having no problem accessing funding in the interbank market. In other words, Barclays wasn't about to run out of cash. The customers aren't going to desert us either, added the executive responsible for looking after the bank's biggest corporate clients.

The only outsider among the furrowed Barclays faces was the bank's senior adviser from Credit Suisse. James Leigh-Pemberton, the straight-talking son of a former governor of the Bank of England, had spent the day on the phone talking to shareholders. They're not happy, but they'll back you, he said, addressing Diamond.

During more than two hours of discussion, nobody seriously raised the possibility that Diamond should leave. The charismatic leader promised to come up with a plan over the weekend, and, as in so many meetings in the room over the years, his troops lined up behind him. If anyone doubted Diamond's ability to survive the firestorm, they kept it to themselves.

As Agius packed up his belongings, he was given a message to call Adair Turner, the chairman of the FSA. The conversation was cordial but clipped. After five minutes Turner broached the issue at the front of both their minds. "Can brand Bob really survive?" he asked. "I don't see why not," replied Agius, before heading to the lift and down to the car waiting for him outside.

■ ■ ■

While London raged, Washington slid lethargically into the holiday season. As hard as the CFTC and the Justice Department tried to get Libor into the public consciousness, the scandal failed to gain much traction with the U.S. media or the country's politicians. In part, it was an issue of timing. The original plan was to settle with Barclays at the start of the month. However, delays at the FSA meant they couldn't push the button until the Wednesday before Independence Day, when most people had one eye on their summer vacation.

There was also the matter of geography. Despite the impact on the dollar and the involvement of a number of American institutions, this was the *London* interbank offered rate, Barclays was a U.K. bank, and the U.S. had enough problems of its own. Stories were starting to emerge about a huge, undisclosed loss at JPMorgan caused by a French trader known in the market as the London Whale on account of the huge positions he took.[12] Libor slipped off the agenda, leaving U.S. investigators with little choice but to put their feet up and watch in amazement as events unfolded on the other side of the Atlantic.

The Saturday after the settlement, those events were focused on a small, exclusive area to the west of central London, where Barclays's two most senior bankers had homes within walking distance of each other. The previous night's board meeting had done little to quell Agius's sense of unease about the future of the bank. After talking it through with his wife Kate, an heiress to the Rothschild banking dynasty, he had begun to wonder whether it might be better if he fell on his sword and stood down.

Diamond, meanwhile, had no such misgivings. The battle-hardened former trader viewed the week's events as part of a longstanding push by his enemies to take him down. He was particularly incensed by the way he felt regulators had treated him. When Diamond was vetted for the CEO job at the end of 2010, the issue of Libor had barely come up; and just two weeks ago he'd attended a meeting at the FSA to discuss a reshuffle at the top of Barclays where the atmosphere was convivial. Over in the U.S., the CFTC had done nothing but praise Barclays's cooperation in the run-up to the settlement. Now it seemed like he couldn't switch on the television or open a newspaper without seeing officials lining up to pour scorn on him and the bank.

That evening Agius made his way to Diamond's residence, an elegant townhouse among the foreign embassies of Belgravia. The two men drank white wine while Diamond laid out the plan he had been working on. Barclays would announce on Monday a review into what had gone wrong, and there would be a new code of conduct for employees to sign.

When Diamond was finished, Agius drained his glass, said goodbye and walked out into the warm night. He didn't mention he was considering resigning. Somehow it didn't seem like the right time.

■ ■ ■

Barclays dominated the front pages again on Sunday, July 1. By now it was clear that the only way to ease the pressure would be for senior personnel to depart. Diamond, who spent the morning strategizing at his house over breakfast with senior non-executive director Mike Rake, had no intention of going anywhere, so, after another fitful night, Agius resolved to leave.

As Rake was driving back to his country residence, he got a call from Agius notifying him of his decision. Rake, like the rest of the board members, tried to talk him out of it, but not too vociferously. Agius was well regarded, but "Diamond Bob" was considered irreplaceable. As Agius sat at his dining table typing his resignation letter, another player in the drama entered from stage left. Jerry Del Missier, who had been with Diamond at Barclays from the start, had been promoted to chief operating officer a week before the Barclays settlement—an appointment approved by the FSA. That Sunday he flew to London from New York to help douse the fire. In reality, he was the lighter fuel.

At 2:33 p.m., the *Financial Times* published an article identifying Diamond and Bank of England Deputy Governor Paul Tucker as the unnamed senior manager and government official referenced in the settlements whose October 2008 call led Barclays staff to believe they'd been ordered to lower their Libor submissions by the central bank.[13] Diamond was no longer just the man in charge when Libor rigging happened. He was directly involved.

When Diamond had got off the phone with Tucker close to four years earlier, the first thing he'd done was call Del Missier. The two men's accounts of that conversation differ, but Del Missier came away with the clear message that Barclays had been told by the Bank of England to start lowballing, which he duly passed down the chain of command.[14] With no record of the Diamond–Tucker conversation beyond an ambiguous memo, the two men had a degree of plausible deniability. Del Missier had no such protection.

Like something out of a gangster movie, it fell to one of Del
Missier's oldest friends to pull the trigger. Ricci, the tweed-suit-wearing,
racehorse-owning Barclays Capital enforcer, arrived at Del Missier's
home that evening and told him he was out. Diamond's mind was made
up. And with that, a 15-year partnership built on friendship and loyalty
came to an end.

By now, Agius's decision to leave instead of Diamond was looking
increasingly incongruous with events, and a board call was lined up for
7 p.m. to discuss whether it was still the best move. But it was too late.
There had been a leak, and minutes before the call was scheduled to take
place, the BBC's business correspondent Robert Peston broke the news.
Diamond and the board had played their hand. All they could do now
was cross their fingers and pray it was enough.

■ ■ ■

In a quiet corner of the open-plan seventh floor at the FSA headquarters
on the morning of Monday July 2, the U.K.'s two most senior regulators
were deep in conversation. At 7 a.m., Barclays had issued a statement
announcing what by that stage everybody knew: Agius was resigning. For
Adair Turner—tall, slim with a lustrous sweep of silver hair—and Andrew
Bailey—shorter, fuller-faced and balding—it represented a conundrum.

Barclays was one of the world's largest and most systemically important financial institutions, and all this uncertainty was destabilizing. Now,
the Bank of England, a pillar of the British establishment, had been
dragged into the muck. Even after Agius's departure, it was unclear
whether Diamond could hold on to his job.

Turner and Bailey were desperate to avoid a situation where Barclays
lost both its CEO and its chairman in one hit. The two men talked
through the options. None was particularly palatable. Can Diamond stay
and ride it out? Does he go and Agius comes back? Maybe Diamond
can announce he'll move on in six months to allow a smooth transition
while Barclays finds a replacement?

Adding to the pressure, both men had just been thrust into new jobs.
Since 2007, the U.K. regulator had been run by Hector Sants, a former
UBS banker with a reputation as a friend to the industry. When the
government announced it was disbanding the agency and devolving its

powers to the Bank of England, Sants agreed to leave. His last day was officially June 29, but in reality he'd taken the last few days as holiday, leaving the previously non-executive chairman, Turner, and Bailey, the head of the Bank of England's new supervisory division, in charge.

The Barclays CEO had made a point of cultivating a good relationship with Sants over the years, dropping in to see the regulator at least once a month.[15] When Diamond had been made group CEO it was Sants who'd signed off on the appointment. Now, just as that relationship might have paid dividends, Sants was on a sun lounger somewhere reading a paperback.

From Diamond's vantage point, it was a cruel blow. Bailey was a hardliner, who had already rebuked Barclays for its laissez-faire approach to regulation at a board meeting earlier in the year.[16] Meanwhile, Turner was on the campaign trail after privately throwing his hat into the ring as a candidate to replace King at the Bank of England. Among his rivals for the post was Tucker.[17]

In the end it wasn't the FSA Diamond needed to worry about. Three blocks away from the FSA's headquarters, Agius was sitting in his office at Barclays, shell-shocked, a picture of stillness amid the chaos around him. The bank was in crisis-management mode, with communications people, lawyers and advisers milling around the executive floor. That morning Del Missier had arrived, flanked by a phalanx of attorneys and unwilling to go down without a fight.[18] Then Agius's phone rang. It was the Bank of England, summoning him and Rake to a meeting with the governor.

It was rush hour when the black town car carrying the two men pulled up outside the Bank of England's imposing, gray-stone façade. Set across an entire block in the heart of the City, the Old Lady of Threadneedle Street is a sprawling hive of marble corridors, grand halls, offices and anterooms. They were led to the governor's quarters, an area known as the parlors, which is attended by doormen in pink tailcoats and top hats.

King was waiting for them in a meeting room dressed in a dark suit and rimless spectacles, his full head of silver hair parted to one side. Apart from a note-taker, the three men were alone. Usually inscrutable, the governor was noticeably agitated.

"I didn't enjoy reading about your resignation from Robert Peston," he snapped, referring to Sunday's leak to the BBC. "The wrong man has gone." Agius had been chairman of Barclays for five years, yet he and King had only had one formal meeting before.

"The chancellor of the exchequer and the head of the FSA both know about this meeting and what I'm about to say," King continued. "I'm not your regulator and I have no power to tell you what to do. But you should know that we no longer have confidence in your CEO."

When Agius pointed out that Diamond had the support of the shareholders, King waived his hand dismissively, brushing his objections away.

"But they own the company!" bristled Rake, a City grandee who also sat on the boards of BT Group and easyJet and was president of the Confederation of British Industry. We were told explicitly by the FSA that they had no problem with his being chief executive, said Agius, trying a different approach.

"Gentlemen, I'm afraid you have been let down by a weak regulator," said King, drawing the conversation to a close.

Agius and Rake walked back to the car in silence. It was a shocking development. The governor of the Bank of England, a man with no direct regulatory power over Barclays, had terminated Diamond's career and consigned the bank to an uncertain future. Worse, in their eyes he had done so to placate public, media and political opinion. For the Barclays executives, it was a betrayal. As the Treasury Select Committee investigating the scandal later concluded: "What many would consider the right decision was taken for the wrong reasons."[19]

It was still light when they arrived at Agius's small second office on Brook Street in Mayfair, where they were met by a second non-executive director, Simon Fraser. Agius relayed the news to a stunned board on a conference call, then telephoned George Osborne to corroborate what King had told them. "We're all of the same view," the chancellor said. A short while later, the board convened a second call and asked Agius to come back and temporarily take the helm. After calling Bailey at the FSA to approve the move, Agius agreed. His resignation had lasted less than two days.

It had been a punishing, heartbreaking day, but it wasn't over yet. At about 10 p.m., Agius and Rake were picked up and driven through the nocturnal London streets to Belgravia. Their mission: to shoot Bob Diamond.

When they arrived, Diamond answered the door and invited them inside. The Barclays CEO had not heard from Agius since he'd left for the Bank of England five hours earlier. He was alone in his vast home, his wife and children away. When Agius finished explaining the decision, Diamond fell silent. Visibly shaken, he stood up, shook the hands of the two men and told them: "I must speak to my family now."

■ ■ ■

Diamond poured himself a glass of water, fixed a smile and told the world: "Wow. I love Barclays. That's where it starts. I love Barclays because of the people."

It was Wednesday, July 4, 2012, and Diamond was sitting alone in the middle of a long desk in a sober navy suit, hands clasped reverentially in front of him. He was face to face with more than a dozen politicians from three different parties who could all smell blood. It was less than 36 hours since the 60-year-old from Concord, Massachusetts, had tendered his resignation. Now he found himself in a packed room across the road from the Houses of Parliament trying to explain what exactly had gone wrong.

"Mr. Diamond, could you remind me of the three founding principles of the Quakers who set up Barclays?" asked John Mann, Labour Party member of parliament for Bassetlaw.

"I can't, sir," said Diamond, rubbing his eyelids.

"I can help, and I could offer to tattoo them on your knuckles if you want, because they are honesty, integrity and plain dealing," said Mann, seizing on the opportunity for a sound bite.

Diamond's mauling was broadcast around the world. It came 16 years to the day after he joined Barclays on Independence Day 1996. It was a watershed moment, the decimation of a career of almost unparalleled success in British banking and a nadir in the public's perception of banks.

The day before, Barclays had gamely tried to fight back. Shortly after announcing Diamond's resignation, the bank published an exculpatory dossier laying out the dozens of times employees of the firm had attempted to alert the authorities to Libor's flaws—much more than any other institution. It also contained a copy of Diamond's memo to Del Missier and John Varley outlining the 2008 Tucker call, with its loaded suggestion that "it did not always need to be the case that Barclays's submissions were as high as they were".[20] It was, as the *Financial Times* wrote, a "political grenade".[21]

But, when questioned by the committee, Diamond—to the consternation of his friends and colleagues—refused to follow through and lay blame at the feet of the Bank of England and his old friend Tucker. His suggestion that it was all a misunderstanding rang false and, rather than swaying the mood, only served to heighten the public opprobrium: a perfect picture of banks and government in cahoots. Diamond may have resigned, but in the minds of a significant proportion of the British public, he still refused to accept responsibility for what he had done.

Over the next hour and a half, Diamond was hit with more than 300 questions, on everything from Barclays's track record to the fall of Lehman Brothers and the collapse of the Icelandic banking system. Members of his press team winced when he misremembered key events, played up his humble beginnings and, in a bungled attempt at familiarity, referred to committee members by their first names. At that moment Diamond was much more than the CEO of Barclays. He was a symbol for all the misdeeds and recklessness and greed of his profession. Libor had become a byword for corruption.

Chapter 16

The Switcheroo

The knock on Hayes's door came at 7 a.m. on a Tuesday morning two weeks before Christmas 2012. Hayes padded down the bespoke pine staircase of his newly renovated home to let in more than a dozen police officers and Serious Fraud Office investigators. He had been expecting them.[1]

Hayes stood numbly at his wife's side as the officers swept through the property, gathering computers and documents into boxes and loading them into vehicles parked at the end of the gravel driveway. The couple had only moved in a fortnight before. Their infant son was upstairs in bed. Outside, commuters made their way in the dark to the railway station at the bottom of the village.

"You do not have to say anything, but it may harm your defense if you do not mention when questioned something which you later rely on in court," a uniformed officer told Hayes. "Anything you do say may be given in evidence."

Traffic was heavy by the time the former trader was led to the back of a waiting car. The 20-mile crawl from Surrey to the City of London passed in silence.

Bishopsgate police station is a gray, concrete building on one of the financial district's busiest thoroughfares. Set among the packed eateries and shops surrounding Liverpool Street railway station, it's easy to miss. Two doors away, on a wall above a tobacconist, a small mosaic depicting

Sir Robert Peel, the founder of the British police force, looks down on passersby.

It was a fitting location for Hayes's first brush with the authorities. Looming over the street is the London headquarters of Royal Bank of Scotland's Global Banking and Markets division, where Hayes had started his career and where Neil Danziger, Paul White, Brent Davies and Will Hall until recently plied their trade. Dirty Dicks, the RBS traders' haunt, is a block away.

Inside, Hayes was taken to a holding cell, where he came face to face with Terry Farr and a thin man with closely cropped silver hair he didn't recognize. It was James Gilmour, an RP Martin broker who'd occasionally promised to help Hayes by reaching out to his contacts in the market when his boss Farr was away.[2] Despite their current predicament, the two men had never actually met. Farr and Gilmour had been arrested that morning at their homes in Essex. On trial in 2015, Gilmour said he never followed through on his promises and was merely stringing Hayes along. He was acquitted of conspiracy to defraud along with Farr.

Later that day Hayes was taken to a waiting room where Lydia Jonson, his lawyer, was waiting with a lever arch file containing instant messages and transcripts of phone calls between Hayes and his contacts in the market. Hayes had retained a top-tier London firm, Fulcrum Chambers.

Just before 5:30 p.m., Hayes and Jonson were led to a cramped interview room, where they were met by two men from the SFO: Matthew Ball, a senior investigator who had been with the agency for 12 years, and Matthew Chadwick, one of his deputies. Hayes would get to know them well over the weeks ahead.

Since his dismissal from Citigroup at the end of 2010, Hayes had had little contact with the authorities regarding Libor. Rumors circulated about individuals being interviewed and cooperating to save their own skin, and he'd had that discomfiting call with Mirhat, but it was hard to know what to believe. A few months earlier, the FSA had written to Hayes asking him to come in and talk to them, but the meeting had never happened.

With a tape recorder running, Ball told Hayes he had been brought in to answer questions relating to allegations that between 2006 and 2009 he had conspired to manipulate yen Libor with Farr and Gilmour. At that stage, the SFO was focused exclusively on his dealings with RP

Martin. Hayes responded that he planned to help but would need time to consider the 112 pages of evidence so would not be answering any questions that day. It was late when he arrived back in Surrey.

From the moment Barclays settled with regulators on June 27, 2012, sparking a political firestorm that burned for weeks, Hayes's destiny had been leading here. The SFO, which had previously resisted launching a probe into Libor rigging, was forced to reverse its position and on July 6 issued a statement announcing it would be undertaking a criminal investigation. That week the government launched its own review into the scandal.[3] The British public and its politicians were out for scalps.

Unknown to Hayes, the American authorities also had him squarely in their sights. On Dec. 19, eight days after his arrest, Hayes was at home on his computer when a news bulletin popped up with a link to a press conference in Washington.[4] As cameras flashed, Attorney General Eric Holder and Lanny Breuer, head of the Justice Department's criminal division, took turns outlining the $1.5 billion settlement the authorities had reached with UBS over Libor. The Swiss bank, they explained, had pleaded guilty to wire fraud at its Japanese arm. Then came the sucker punch.

"In addition to UBS Japan's agreement to plead guilty, two former UBS traders—Tom Alexander William Hayes and Roger Darin—have been charged, in a criminal complaint unsealed today, with conspiracy to manipulate Libor," said Breuer. "Hayes has also been charged with wire fraud and an antitrust violation."

At that moment the full horror of the situation hit Hayes for the first time.

The two most powerful lawyers in the U.S. planned to extradite him on three separate criminal charges, each carrying a 20–30 year sentence. The fact that Darin was named as a co-conspirator added a sense of the surreal: The two men loathed one another. Sarah, who was making dinner, vomited when she heard the news.[5]

Less than 24 hours later a member of Hayes's legal team was on the phone to the SFO to discuss cutting a deal. Sentences for white-collar crime in the U.S. have historically dwarfed those dished out in the U.K. Fighting the charges seemed futile: The UBS settlement made reference to more than 2,000 attempts by Hayes and his colleagues to influence the rate over a four-year period. He was the star attraction, the "Jesse James of Libor", as he would later tell it.[6] The U.S. authorities had yet to issue extradition papers, but it was only a matter of time.

So began a race to convince the SFO to take on Hayes as a sort of chief informant, the witness in a case who confesses everything and gives up everyone in exchange for leniency and, more importantly, an agreement that he would be dealt with in the U.K.

The SFO had its own agenda. Founded in 1987, the London-based white-collar prosecutor was referred to in some circles as the "Serious Flawed Office" after a string of botched investigations. Two months earlier the agency was forced to drop a three-year probe into the investments of Iranian property magnates, Robert and Vincent Tchenguiz, for lack of evidence of wrongdoing. Its decision the previous year not to launch an investigation into Libor despite clear signs of criminality was now being widely criticized.

Factions within the ruling Conservative government were pushing to have the agency disbanded. With such intense focus on Libor, it was essential that the SFO's new boss, David Green, a former criminal barrister, get his arms around the investigation.

The first week after the Christmas break, Hayes's lawyers met with senior managers from the SFO to discuss their options. Both sides agreed that a U.K. prosecution was the best outcome. The problem was fending off the Americans. The day after Hayes was arrested, the Justice Department had quietly filed criminal charges against him, effectively staking its own claim to the former trader. U.S. authorities had been given no forewarning about his arrest and were furious with what they saw as a brazen attempt by their U.K. counterparts to steal their primary target from under their noses.[7]

From the SFO's point of view, Hayes was a British citizen accused of rigging the London interbank offered rate and should therefore be tried in the U.K. Beyond that, it looked like a slam-dunk case to silence the critics. For the U.S. it was about more than jurisdiction. The SFO's investigation was built entirely on evidence gathered by the U.S. authorities. The U.K. prosecutor had arrived at the party uninvited at five to midnight and was drinking all the booze.

While this transatlantic tug of war was going on, Hayes and his family were in a state of limbo. The SFO was unwilling to contact the Justice Department for fear of alerting them to Hayes's imminent cooperation.

But it wasn't prepared to sign Hayes up to its whistleblower program until it was assured of his value. Each day brought fresh speculation that extradition papers were imminent. The constant threat left Hayes depressed, even suicidal.[8] He couldn't sleep and was unable to focus on basic tasks like driving without losing track of what he was doing.

Desperate to wrest back some control, Hayes agreed to meet David Enrich, an American journalist at *The Wall Street Journal*, in a café by a London tube station. Hayes gambled that the reporter could help his cause by switching the focus from him to his bosses. Enrich published a series of articles in the following weeks laying out Hayes's version of events and highlighting the complicity of his managers.[9] Unknown to the trader's lawyers, the pair remained in close contact.

"I was basically at that point in time pretty much having a breakdown," Hayes later testified. "I was basically living life then on a sort of 24-hour time horizon. Just how do you get through it? How do you survive?"

The solution came in the form of the U.K.'s Serious Organised Crime and Police Act of 2005. SOCPA, as it's commonly known, includes a provision that allows prosecutors to strike a deal with a cooperating witness who assists in the investigation or prosecution of offenses committed by others. In the British law enforcement community it's known as a "supergrass" agreement—slang for snitch.

In order to be admitted to the program, Hayes had to agree to tell the SFO everything he knew and promise to testify against everybody involved. Crucially, he also had to plead guilty to dishonestly rigging Libor. It was not enough to admit trying to influence the rate. He had to confess that he knew it was wrong.

During two days of so-called scoping interviews to test his knowledge, Hayes talked openly about his campaign to rig Libor for the first time in his life. At the SFO's offices near Trafalgar Square he admitted he had acted dishonestly and brought the investigators' attention to aspects of the case they knew nothing about, such as his relationship with Guillaume Adolph at Deutsche Bank.

It was enough to convince the SFO. On March 27, 2013, Hayes was admitted to the program. While the agency couldn't offer Hayes any ironclad promises, the development almost guaranteed he would be dealt with in the U.K. He was driving when his phone rang to notify him of the news. Pulling over, he later recalled, he felt like a man who thought he had terminal cancer and is given the all clear.

There followed a period of intense unburdening. Hayes handed over his passport and was instructed to sleep at his house and sign in at a local police station every Monday—something he regularly forgot to do.[10] For two months, his life eased into a familiar routine. At least once a week, sometimes more, he would make his way to the SFO's offices at 10 a.m. for a day of interviews. After signing in as 1970s Queens Park Rangers legend Stan Bowles,[11] he took the elevator to the fourth floor, walked past the vending machines and stepped into his confessional: a stark white room with a desk, a projector, his lawyer and at least two investigators.

The interviews covered everything from his entry into the industry and his trading strategies to how the Libor scheme began and the various individuals who helped him rig the rate. They barely had to prod to get him to talk. Hayes seemed to relish reliving moments from his past. His voice sped up when he talked about heady days piling into positions, squeezing the best prices from brokers and playing traders off against each other.

"The first thing you think is where's the edge, where can I make a bit more money, how can I push, push the boundaries, maybe you know a bit of a gray area, push the edge of the envelope," he said in one early interview. "But the point is, you are greedy, you want every little bit of money that you can possibly get because, like I say, that is how you are judged, that is your performance metric."

Paper coffee cups piled up as Hayes went over the minutiae of the case: how to hedge a forward rate agreement; the nuances of Libor and Tibor; why he and Darin hated each other so much. One of the interviews was conducted in the dark so Hayes could talk the investigators through his trading book, which was beamed onto a wall. At one stage, Hayes was asked about how he viewed his attempts to move Libor around. The exchange would prove crucial.

"Well look, I mean, it's a dishonest scheme, isn't it? And I was part of the dishonest scheme, so obviously I was being dishonest," Hayes said.

"At the time that the conduct took place…so say starting from Sept. 29, 2006," one of the investigators began. "Do you think you knew at that point, that what you…"

"Well, I mean, I think you're talking about degrees of dishonesty," Hayes interrupted. "I mean I hadn't really sat down and thought, well, when Libor was set up what was the purpose of Libor. So did I think I was going to get a medal from the regulator for doing it? Well, no, I didn't…and if I gave it any thought, I probably thought if this was something that if someone were to look at it from the outside, like a regulator or something, they would be like oh, you know, this is a bit dodgy."

On June 11, after 11 sessions spanning 82 hours, it was over. Hayes had identified more than 20 co-conspirators, including his stepbrother and some of his oldest friends in the market. He'd told prosecutors much more than they had ascertained on their own, going further than what the CFTC, the Justice Department and the FSA had gleaned in years. A week later, Hayes returned to Bishopsgate police station where he was formally charged with conspiracy to defraud. As far as the SFO was concerned, the case was bombproof.

■ ■ ■

Back in Woldingham, Hayes was having trouble sleeping. Any relief he felt at avoiding extradition was replaced by a gnawing sense of injustice. Over the course of his confession, investigators had shown him pieces of evidence he couldn't get out of his mind. There was a heat wave outside, but Hayes spent his days at his kitchen table poring over documents that served to convince him, not of the strength of the case against him, but of the unfairness of it all: e-mails from senior managers applauding his efforts; transcripts that showed manipulation predating his hiring; evidence of UBS's lowballing during the crisis.

Hayes had always maintained that he only made requests for Libor movements within a boundary of where cash would realistically be trading—what his lawyers described as "a permissible range". If he'd asked a trader at another firm to ramp his submission by several basis points, Hayes said, his reputation in the market would have been undermined. Yet the documents showed that his managers had ordered much more significant distortions of the rate.

Hayes fixated on one particular piece of evidence. "Publishing Libor Rates" was a guide stored on UBS's communal hard drive for the

London-based individuals who set Libor in euros and dollars. The file contained the following passage:

> "If this sheet shows a total of over 10k for IBANK/LIBOR, we need to make changes to fixings on Euro Libors new spreadsheet. For example, if 3m Libor is 4.124 this means we are receiving delta Libor/Libor fixing and…we want to increase the fixing by 25 bps. If the number is negative then vice versa." [12]

Forget what managers did or didn't know. To Hayes's mind, here was a black-and-white directive for employees to adjust their Libor submissions according to the bank's derivatives positions. It was, he said, an instruction manual for rigging Libor. "I was burning with rage," Hayes recalled. "I was feeling like I'd been forced into this situation through circumstance and actually…this wasn't a fair deal for me."

By now Hayes's wife had grown so sick of her husband's moods that she gave him an ultimatum: Either accept the situation or get a second opinion. If not, she warned, she would divorce him. [13]

His first port of call was David Bermingham, one of the so-called NatWest Three extradited to the U.S. a decade earlier after pleading guilty to wire fraud related to the Enron scandal. The British banker, who spent more than two years in U.S. and U.K. prisons, told Hayes to resolve matters with the U.S. authorities, lest he spend the rest of his life in fear they would come after him. [14]

Unconvinced, Hayes continued to seek out advice. In the weeks leading up to his arrest another former UBS trader, Kweku Adoboli, was defending himself against allegations of fraud. Adoboli, the son of a Ghanaian diplomat, was arrested in 2011 after racking up losses of $2.3 billion and attempting to hide them using secret, unauthorized accounts. Like Hayes, Adoboli claimed he was taking the rap for the sins of a corrupt organization.

On Nov. 20, 2012, Adoboli was found guilty of two counts of fraud but acquitted of four counts of false accounting. It was something of a reprieve considering he'd nearly brought down the bank. He was sentenced to seven years in prison and would be out in less than three. Hayes contacted Adoboli's barrister, Charles Sherrard, to discuss his case. [15] In the end he didn't retain Sherrard, but the conversation proved pivotal.

If Adoboli could beat some of the charges against him, Hayes reasoned, maybe he could too?

A few weeks later, one afternoon in the middle of August, investigators at the SFO were busy on the case when they received an e-mail notifying them that Hayes had changed lawyers. No longer able to afford the elite Fulcrum Chambers, he had switched to Garstangs Burrows Bussin, a firm that started life in Bolton in the north of England and had just a handful of partners. Unlike Fulcrum, Garstangs accepted clients on legal aid, a British government program that provides representation to people who couldn't otherwise afford it. The permatanned lead partner on the case, Richard Cornthwaite, is described in the Chambers Guide to U.K. attorneys as "a good, steady pair of hands". Somehow those hands had landed one of the biggest white-collar cases in history.

Alarm bells rang at the SFO, but there was no outright panic. It wasn't uncommon for well-paid finance professionals to be forced into downgrading their legal representation when the fees racked up. Then, on Oct. 9, an envelope arrived in the late morning post containing a letter from Hayes's new representatives.

"Mr. Hayes will plead not guilty to all counts," said the brief note. "Accordingly, he now formally withdraws from the SOCPA process."

After seeing off the threat of extradition, Hayes was having one last throw of the dice, sacrificing any leniency he might have received. The SFO case team was stunned. They had a deal! What the hell was he playing at? Without Hayes's testimony the whole case could be in jeopardy. They hit straight back, issuing an order freezing Hayes's assets and limiting his spending to £250 a week. He had already transferred ownership of the house to Sarah, who took out a £350,000 mortgage to cover the mounting legal bills.[16]

"I have no idea what the jury will decide," Hayes would later say, explaining the last-minute switch. "But, you know what, I would rather that 12 people made their mind up about me than I plead guilty to a politically driven process which I'm forced into by the actions of a government that has nothing to do with Japan or Japanese interest rates and a politically driven process on this side of the Atlantic."[17]

The battle lines were drawn.

Chapter 17

The Trial

On May 26, 2015, Hayes gritted his teeth and walked nervously past a packed gallery to take his seat in Courtroom Two of Southwark Crown Court, an austere 1980s brown brick cube on the south bank of the Thames. Directly across the river the high-rise towers of the City of London dominate the skyline.

Dressed in chinos, a black sweater and no tie, freshly shaven, his hair newly cut, the first person to stand trial globally for rigging Libor looked a long way from the aggressive, controlling bully the prosecution would paint him to be. His petite mother, wearing an elegant silk scarf, shrunk into her reserved seat among the press pack.

That morning photographers had jostled to capture Hayes and his wife as they made their way into the building. White vans sprouting satellite dishes lined the streets. Hayes's image was beamed onto TV screens and plastered across the front pages of newspapers around the world.

It was more than seven years after McGonagle and his colleagues at the CFTC had started probing Libor and 18 months since Hayes's arrest. It had been a difficult period. After early success trading for himself, Hayes's fortunes had nosedived and he'd lost close to a million pounds.[1] Tighe had been forced to go back to work and for a few weeks they separated. They rented out the Old Rectory to generate some income and were now living with their young son in a modest, rented house near Tighe's parents in Hampshire. Hayes's hair was starting to turn gray and he'd begun chain-smoking.[2]

Hayes and his team of solicitors and barristers occupied the left half of the long desks in the middle of the courtroom on entering, while the prosecution took the right side. All faced the judge, who sat elevated behind a dais at the front in red robes with white woolen trim that matched the color of his ceremonial wig. The jury was seated at two rows of desks along the left wall, facing the witness stand on the opposite side of the room. Reporters, lawyers and onlookers took up the 50 or so seats in the public gallery at the back.

The judge, Justice Jeremy Cooke, was a 66-year-old former professional rugby player with a fearsome reputation. A member of the evangelical Lawyers' Christian Fellowship, he attracted controversy in 2012 when he sentenced a woman to eight years in prison for performing a late-stage abortion on herself. Before Hayes's trial began, counsel for the defense had tried to have him removed for demonstrating bias against their client. Cooke had commented in a hearing that he couldn't see why, with so much evidence against Hayes, the trial would take more than a couple of weeks.

The seven men and five women of the jury, many of whom were drawn from the predominantly working-class surrounding area, shuffled into the courtroom through their own side entrance just before 11 a.m. Because of Hayes's Asperger's diagnosis, made three months before, he was granted permission to sit with his legal team rather than alone in the dock—an enclosed glass box in the center of the courtroom that quickly became prime real estate for journalists. He was also given an intermediary who sat next to him throughout the trial, monitoring his demeanor for signs of stress and mouthing "calm down" when he became agitated. Hayes would need constant attention, shaking his head wildly and jumping up from his seat to pass scribbled notes to his lawyers when he heard something he didn't like.

Representing the SFO was chief prosecutor Mukul Chawla QC, an amiable bear of a man in a black robe with thick silver hair and an e-cigarette he puffed on during breaks in spite of numerous signs prohibiting it.[3] Chawla, a Bruce Springsteen fan who rode to court on a motorbike, had been a criminal barrister for more than 30 years and a silk, the top tier of the profession, for about half that time. In 2012, he had successfully defended the head of derivatives brokerage Blue Index against charges of insider trading brought by the U.K. financial regulator. It was an embarrassment for the FSA. One of the only other times it had lost an insider-dealing case was in 2010, when Chawla was again part of the defense team. Unwilling to risk a black eye at his agency, SFO head David Green called Chawla at his London chambers the week the agency announced its Libor investigation in July 2012 and asked him to front the prosecution. Chawla, who was born in Nairobi to Indian parents and was raised not far from where Hayes grew up in West London, knew it would mean months toiling into the night, rarely seeing his wife and two daughters. But he couldn't refuse. It was one the biggest fraud cases in a generation.

For the first four days, Chawla laid out the case against Hayes in soft, measured tones. "The prosecution never needs to prove the motive for the crime, but you may think, having heard the evidence, that here the motive was a simple one," he said during his opening address. "It was greed. Mr. Hayes's desire was to earn and to make as much money as he could. The more that he earned for his employers, the more they would value his services and inevitably, he hoped, the more that they would pay him."

Chawla advised the jury to look beyond the jargon and the complexity of the evidence and recognize Hayes's behavior for what he argued it was: a simple case of cheating. "In essence," the prosecutor said, looking into the eyes of the jurors one by one, "it is little different to agreeing with someone to nobble a horse and betting on the outcome of the race which you have now rigged in your favor."

There was no disputing what Hayes had done. Thousands of e-mails, instant chats and telephone recordings of him asking traders and brokers for help moving the rate were presented by the prosecution in painstaking detail over long, airless days, which hammered home the sheer industry and single-mindedness of his endeavors. But what the prosecution needed to demonstrate, if the eight counts of fraud against him were to stand up, was that Hayes knew what he was doing was dishonest.

The test for dishonesty in British law has two legs and derives from the 1982 trial of a surgeon named Dr. Deb Baran Ghosh, who was accused of inflating his hours and fiddling his fees. The appeal court judge in the case said jurors must decide whether an ordinary, decent person would consider an action dishonest and, if so, whether the accused himself considered his behavior to be dishonest. Both parts must be satisfied. The prosecution's greatest weapons were the former trader's own words.

"I knew that, you know, I probably shouldn't do it," Hayes told investigators during his first full interview with the SFO on Jan. 31, 2013, which was played through the court's speakers at a high enough volume that they started to distort. "But, like I said, I was participating in an industrywide practice."

"I probably deserve to be sitting here," he said later in the same series of interviews. "Ultimately, I was someone who was a serial offender."

Arguing for the defense was Neil Hawes, a small, wiry barrister with black hair and milk-bottle-lens glasses, who was drafted onto the case late when Hayes dropped his previous representative months before the trial.[4] Hawes was an experienced trial lawyer with a bookish countenance who had built a reputation advising government agencies on complex fraud cases. Each morning, he scurried purposefully and silently into court with an armful of folders and his head down. During breaks in proceedings he locked himself away with his team and members of Hayes's family in a tiny anteroom. Chawla, by contrast, always made a point of stopping to talk to the press. At one stage his team handed out sweets to the court staff and opposition counsel.

The case for the defense was threefold: First, that much of the communication that made up the evidence against Hayes had been misconstrued and was in fact perfectly innocent; second, that Hayes only sought to have the rate moved within a permissible range of where cash might actually trade; and third, that influencing Libor was so pervasive—so widely practiced and accepted and so poorly policed—that Hayes could not have realized that what he was doing was wrong. Hawes took the jury through the evidence methodically, with the air of a university professor who no longer has much enthusiasm for his material.

All three arguments carried significant problems. It was difficult for Hayes to claim now that the e-mails and chats in which he appeared to be discussing rigging the rate were innocuous, when he had openly and repeatedly described them as anything but to the SFO two years earlier. He was either lying then or lying now, neither of which created a favorable impression.

And the notion of a permissible range had no basis in law. The BBA rules dictated that banks were forbidden from taking into consideration their trading positions when submitting to Libor, so Hayes requesting only small, almost imperceptible movements was of no consequence—even if the submissions he and his co-conspirators sought were reasonable estimates of their banks' borrowing costs at the time. It's a peculiar irony of the case that Hayes may have sometimes made the rate more accurate through his interference.

The third argument—that Libor-rigging was standard practice across the industry—seemed to have more mileage. Almost a dozen firms had been sanctioned for failing to control their traders, yet so far Hayes was the only individual to be dragged before a judge. At UBS, Hawes demonstrated, traders had been basing their submissions on their derivatives positions long before Hayes arrived on the scene. And at Citigroup, managers discussed how they could move the rate during the crisis—although there were no signs they acted on it. It was also clear that some of Hayes's bosses encouraged his behavior. Among the most compelling pieces of evidence was the 2009 e-mail sent by Hayes's former boss Pieri citing the trader's influence over the "rate-setters in London" as a reason to offer him a bigger bonus. Shortly after receiving the message, Carsten Kengeter, UBS's head of investment banking at the time, approved a significant bump in Hayes's pay.[5]

However, as Chawla pointed out in his opening remarks, the blessing of his employer was no defense in the eyes of the law. In UBS, Hayes had joined a firm with a deep-seated culture of corruption, but he'd also gone further than anyone else.[6] Before he arrived, nobody at the bank had considered enlisting the brokers or routinely leaning on traders at other institutions for favors. When Hayes started doing it, his bosses were delighted with the results, but it was the trader's ingenuity, not his employer's.

Besides, Hayes may have been the first, but he wouldn't be the last to be hauled into a courtroom. At least a dozen other traders and brokers had been lined up to face trial in the U.K. and the U.S., while another six had pleaded guilty and were awaiting sentencing. Privately, the SFO was promising to charge more of Hayes's network in the coming months.

During the third week, Hawes was given the opportunity to cross-examine John Ewan, the former director responsible for Libor at the

BBA. His goal was to demonstrate that the organization responsible for overseeing the benchmark was so complicit in its abuse and so lax in its oversight that it was wrong to single out any individual traders for their behavior. Just before lunchtime on June 5, Ewan made his way to the stand dressed in a pinstriped suit, bobbing his head anxiously.

The BBA had been stripped of responsibility for Libor in September 2013 following condemnation over its failure to police the rate.[7] Ewan had left the organization the previous year to join Thomson Reuters. To the end, he and his colleagues maintained that they didn't know for sure that banks were lowballing Libor during the crisis and that they hadn't considered the possibility that traders were moving the benchmark around to boost their profits.

After swearing an oath, Ewan was taken through a series of e-mails, phone calls and documents from his time at the trade body. What emerged over the next four excruciating days was an institution that was comically inept, almost certainly dishonest, and which ultimately bears as much responsibility for one of the worst episodes of market abuse as any trader.

The tone was set early on, when Ewan was asked if he knew that banks were lowballing their submissions during the crisis. "We would hear repeated allegations," he answered, his gangly frame leaning forward in his chair, but there "were never actual smoking guns".

The jury was then shown the first in a long series of smoking guns: a transcript of the April 2008 call in which Barclays executive Miles Storey, the chairman of the BBA's Libor committee at the time, called Ewan and suggested that his bank was inputting dollar rates 10 basis points lower than where they should be. "No one's clean-clean now," Ewan had replied.

Next, the jury was played the conversation in which Ewan and Storey discussed the BBA's plan to get the dollar Libor panel banks to increase their submissions simultaneously. "So the idea is," Ewan said on the 2008 call, his words reverberating around the courtroom, "to see if we can gradually float the dollar rate slightly, gently up."

Asked to elucidate on the recording, Ewan looked down for an uncomfortably long period of time before replying indignantly: "I don't accept that there was necessarily any central strategy to try and float the dollars up," drawing exasperated sniggers from the gallery.

The former BBA director was just as entrenched on the subject of whether he knew that traders like Hayes were manipulating the rates to maximize their profits, claiming he only realized it was possible when he read Barclays's settlement with the CFTC in June 2012. E-mails and minutes starting seven years earlier appeared to contradict that position.

"Many institutions set their Libors based on their derivative reset positions," a Bank of Scotland trader wrote to Ewan in one December 2007 e-mail shown to jurors. Another message, this one from a BNP Paribas employee, cited the example of "a large Swiss bank whose Libors are quoted by its interest rate swaps desk," concluding: "That puts their pricing for Libor against the off balance-sheet positions and has nothing to do with cash."

At one point the jury heard a call in which Ewan recounted to Storey how he had been contacted by an executive from Middle Eastern lender Gulf International Bank, who said he had evidence that a rate-setting bank was offering cash in the market at much higher rates than it was submitting. Rather than investigating the matter, Ewan told Storey he opted not to ask the name of the offending institution.

"Why did you specifically ask him not to name the bank?" Hawes asked him in court.

"I don't recall exactly," Ewan replied after several seconds, "but I think it would have been because I would not have known what my response or responsibility should have been without speaking to my management, the Foreign Exchange and Money Markets Committee." Without, in other words, speaking to the very individuals who worked for the banks accused of rigging the rate.

Accounting for his actions, Ewan said that the BBA had consistently attempted to ensure the accuracy of the Libor rate during exceptional circumstances, and pointed out that he had passed on any concerns about potential manipulation to his managers. He added that the BBA had no regulatory power and that both the Bank of England and the FSA were unwilling to take a more active role in overseeing the rate at the time.

Ewan walked off the stand and out of the courtroom on June 10, looking dazed. What was left of the BBA's credibility was in tatters. The problem for the defense was that the Libor administrator's laxity did not expunge Hayes's behavior. A burglar is no less guilty, Chawla told the jury, "because the householder has left a window open for him to enter".

After representatives from UBS and Citigroup were questioned, Hayes was finally called to give evidence on the morning of July 7. Before he entered, the judge told the jurors about his Asperger's. The disorder, which had been diagnosed by a court-approved psychiatrist, did not affect Hayes's ability to distinguish between honest and dishonest acts, Cooke said, but may help explain the nature of his answers. The courtroom was full to capacity. Dressed in a gray sweater, with one hand in his trouser pocket, Hayes walked past his wife, mother and stepfather and took his seat on the witness stand, facing the jurors. He placed a photograph of his son in front of him.

The first three days were spent answering questions from his own counsel, who asked him to comment on a succession of e-mails and instant messages that appeared to show him attempting to move the rate. Hayes said the fact he had discussed Libor so openly was evidence he did not think he was doing anything wrong. He had been given next to no training and was not dishonest, he claimed, because the practice of trying to influence Libor was so common it never occurred to him that he couldn't do it. Hayes's counsel sought to back up his claims with documents showing him brushing off warnings from his alleged co-conspirators about investigations into Libor as "a non-story", and even updating his Facebook status with messages like: "Tom needs a low 1m Libor".

Asked why he had provided hours of detailed testimony only to change his mind, Hayes said he felt he had no other option. At the time he was suicidal, he said, and unable to make rational decisions.

"My main concern was whether I was going to be put on a plane to the USA within the next seven days," Hayes told the court. "All I knew at that point was I couldn't go in and say I had done nothing wrong so I knew that there were going to be very tricky parts of the interview which I was concerned about because I knew that if I had, you know, been allowed to answer as I wished, then the answers would have been different."

At one point Hayes broke down in tears, exclaiming, "I don't think I've done anything," then looking over at Tighe, who sat in the gallery in a shirt buttoned to the collar, her blonde hair tied back neatly and her hands clasped in her lap. She nodded back in support. When the prosecution played audio clips of Hayes joking around with his contacts in the market, he laughed to himself.

"It could be the worst job in the world," Hayes said on the stand. "It could make you want to jump off a bridge and it can make you feel physically sick every time you went into work." Still, one of the hardest things about his current situation, he explained, was that he was no longer allowed to trade. "I was and to a lesser degree am now still obsessed with the markets, the financial markets, and very, very, very much miss my old job. I very much miss my old career. It was a big, big part of my identity, that job and that career for me."

By the end of his first week on the stand, what had begun as an open-and-shut-case was starting to slip away from Chawla. The young man being presented by the defense was straightforward, sincere, maybe even a little naïve—as much a victim of the system as the perpetrator of a crime.

Any hope Hayes allowed himself over the weekend drained dramatically during his cross-examination on Monday morning. Asked to confirm basic facts, such as what instruments he traded, he turned evasive and combative. When Chawla asked what Read had meant when he described the rate-setters at other banks as "sheep", Hayes replied "a four-legged animal". When the prosecutor suggested his initial cooperation with the SFO was "nothing more than a charade", he shot back: "My idea of charades is a game that's played at Christmas."

Chawla continued to probe Hayes on the evidence against him. Rather than addressing the prosecutor's questions, Hayes tried to change the subject, decrying the investigation as lacking any rigorous analysis and claiming he was a victim of a struggle for supremacy between U.K. and U.S. authorities—a "fugitive from American justice". Visibly, he tensed up, clenching his jaw and narrowing his eyes. At one point he claimed that all his efforts to rig Libor had been unsuccessful, citing his own examination of the trading data. Eventually, the judge intervened, telling Hayes to answer the questions and refrain from making speeches.

Ten weeks after the trial began, the jury was sent away to deliberate. After five days, it returned a unanimous verdict: Guilty on all counts. Half an hour later, Hayes walked back into the packed, hushed courtroom for the final time. On this occasion he couldn't avoid the dock. Before entering, he asked a uniformed guard if he could kiss his wife goodbye. Dressed in a blue shirt and light blue sweater and carrying an overnight bag, he was led into the glass cell. The door was locked behind him.

Hayes barely reacted when the judge announced he would be imprisoned for 14 years, a sentence at the highest end of the spectrum for white-collar criminals in the U.K. His wife shook her head, bent forward and grasped the arm of Hayes's mother, who stared straight ahead, silently shaking.

"What you did, with others, was dishonest, as you well appreciated at the time," the judge said in his closing remarks. "What this case has shown is the absence of that integrity which ought to characterize banking."

Hayes was no longer listening. When the judge finished speaking, he was led from the dock to the basement of Southwark Crown Court, past the holding cells and into the back of an armored van. From there he was driven through the London traffic to Wandsworth Prison, the imposing 19th-century jail where he would see out the first days of his sentence.

Afterword

ollowing a 2012 review, the process for setting Libor was overhauled. Responsibility for managing the rate was stripped from the British Bankers' Association and handed to a subsidiary of the New York Stock Exchange, which promised to keep a closer eye on banks' submissions. Libor-setting is now a regulated activity, and the law has been amended to make it a standalone criminal offense to attempt to manipulate Libor or any other financial benchmark.

Still, many question whether Libor can survive. The market for unsecured short-term loans—the whole underpinning of the Libor system—never really recovered after the financial crisis, meaning the rates the banks provide remain largely the product of guesswork. The Federal Reserve has established a committee of banks and regulators to help come up with alternative benchmarks on which to peg the trillions of dollars of derivatives and loans that still rely on Libor. After three years, they are no closer to arriving at an agreement.

Hayes appealed both his conviction and the length of his sentence, and on Dec. 1, 2015, a hearing was held at London's Royal Courts of Justice. For three days his lawyers argued to have his sentence overturned on the grounds that Justice Cooke had instructed jurors not to take into account the prevalence of Libor-rigging in financial markets when assessing Hayes's actions. They also claimed Cooke had refused to admit key evidence. Hayes was absent for the proceedings.

The three-person appellate panel, which included John Thomas, the U.K.'s most senior judge, upheld the conviction in a written statement a week before Christmas. They did, however, reduce Hayes's sentence from 14 years to 11, saying it was "excessive" given his age, seniority and Asperger's condition. Hayes, who maintains his innocence, immediately filed to have the case heard by the British supreme court but was rejected. He was ordered to pay back £878,806 determined to be the proceeds of crime. He is currently residing at Lowdham Grange, a modern, 920-inmate prison in Nottinghamshire in central England. Under British rules, he could serve less than six years. His family have launched a campaign to help fund a fresh review by the Criminal Cases Review Commission, an independent organization set up to investigate miscarriages of justice.

The six interdealer brokers accused of colluding with Hayes— Darrell Read, Colin Goodman and Danny Wilkinson from ICAP; Terry Farr and James Gilmour from RP Martin; and Noel Cryan, who worked at Tullett Prebon—were tried in the same courtroom as Hayes over three months starting Oct. 6, 2015.

The SFO was confident going into the proceedings. ICAP and RP Martin had already admitted wrongdoing and been fined a combined $90 million by the CFTC and the FCA. There were several thousand e-mails, instant-message chats and recorded phone calls that seemed to indicate the men's involvement in the scheme, much of it the exact same evidence used to convict Hayes. Together, they admitted receiving more than £450,000 in kickbacks. One of the brokers, Farr, even acknowledged leaning on his clients to change their submissions, arguing that he didn't know he wasn't allowed to and therefore hadn't acted dishonestly.

Yet it was a separate case, with fresh facts and a different jury. Conspiracy to defraud in U.K. law occurs when two or more people strike an agreement to dishonestly deprive another of something. The SFO had to demonstrate, beyond reasonable doubt, that the defendants had not only agreed with Hayes to get banks to change their submissions but also intended to follow through on that agreement and had known it was dishonest at the time.

Aside from Farr, the men all said that they had fobbed Hayes off. They described him as a nightmare client with a "god complex" who made their lives hell. Cryan said he had duped Hayes from the start, taking the credit when Libor moved the trader's way and ignoring his calls when it didn't. Read suggested that the hundreds of e-mails and texts he'd sent Goodman asking him to change his run-through were nothing more than information-sharing. Goodman testified that he'd lied to the badgering Read when he wrote back promising to help. Wilkinson and Gilmour maintained they barely knew Hayes and had very little to do with him.

The SFO didn't help itself. The agency had compiled a schedule of days on which it claimed rigging had taken place, but under cross-examination it emerged that several of the dates were wrong. In some cases, the defendants had been on holiday. At one point a barrister for one of the defendants turned to the jurors and described the SFO's case as a "complete shambles".

Chawla again urged the jurors to forget the financial terminology and the esoteric nature of the evidence, but before the first day was out he'd used words like "derivatives", "interest-rate swaps" and "ISDA definitions". By day four, one of the jurors had fallen asleep. Others followed suit as the trial progressed.

Defense counsel portrayed the brokers as simple family men at the lowest rungs of the financial-industry ladder who had already paid a heavy price. One afternoon, jurors returned from lunch to find an empty chair in the dock. Wilkinson had been taken to the hospital and was unable to attend the remainder of the trial. A few days before, red-faced and sweating, he'd appeared desperate when he took the stand.

On Jan. 27, 2016, just a day after they were sent away to deliberate, the jurors returned a unanimous verdict for everyone except Read: not guilty. The following morning, with his co-defendants looking on from the gallery, the former ICAP broker was also acquitted, this time by a majority vote. Of the more than 20 individuals identified by Hayes as taking part in the scheme, he is the only one to be convicted.

Gary Gensler has left the CFTC and helped manage the financial side of Hillary Clinton's election campaign. Vince McGonagle and

Gretchen Lowe are still with the agency, unearthing corruption with limited resources. Steve Obie is working in private practice with law firm Jones Day. Anne Termine joined Lanny Breuer and Eric Holder at Covington & Burling.

Two years after leaving Barclays, Bob Diamond returned to the fray in 2014 with a new venture, Atlas Mara, which invests in banks in Africa. Paul Tucker is now a senior fellow at Harvard University.

Epilogue: The Wild West

In the spring of 2013, while Tom Hayes was spilling his guts in a cramped interrogation room, we were across town in the wood-paneled dining area of The Old Doctor Butler's Head, a spit-and-sawdust pub nestled in an alleyway in the City of London. Across the table, nursing a mineral water, his eyes darting anxiously, was an executive from one of Europe's biggest fund managers. A few weeks earlier, as Libor blew through the U.K. like a tornado, he'd called the Bloomberg newsroom with a tip.

"I don't have any proof," the fund manager explained when we asked him to take us through it one more time. "But I'm positive there's something wrong with the 4 p.m. fix. There has to be."

The 4 p.m. fix is a currency benchmark set each afternoon in London that's every bit as pervasive in global financial markets as Libor. It's a once-a-day snapshot of exchange rates used to calculate the value of trillions of dollars of investments. FTSE and MSCI, for example, calculate their indexes using the rates. It can also determine how much money asset managers get when they swap one currency for another.

The big difference between the 4 p.m. fix and Libor is that it's based on actual trades rather than bank estimates. At the time of the meeting,

WM/Reuters, the company that runs the benchmark, tracked currency trading over a 60-second period from 15:59:30 to 16:00:30, then calculated an average.[1] The process was used for 150 exchange rates: everything from euro-dollar to dollar-Bangladeshi taka.[2]

For technical reasons, the fund manager—like major investors all over the world—exchanged billions of dollars at the fix, particularly at month-end, so he scrutinized the numbers closely.[3] Ever since Libor, he'd been feeling suspicious. The rates he got at the fix never seemed to match the prevailing prices in the market around the same time. There were also weird spikes in currencies in the half hour or so before 4 p.m.—the kind of big, one-way moves you might expect to see if banks had found a way to push the market around to rig the benchmark.

The fund manager had raised his concerns at a meeting with the U.K. regulator, but nobody called him back. Although he had no evidence, what he was suggesting was, on the face of it, pretty shocking. Over the past few months, banks had been hit with multibillion dollar fines for rigging Libor, seriously denting their profits. They'd signed deferred prosecution agreements, leaving them facing criminal charges if they stepped out of line again. Dozens of traders had been sacked. Barclays had lost its CEO. The U.K. government had launched an inquiry into standards in banking overseen by the Archbishop of Canterbury. In the U.S., executives from the New York Fed had been dragged before the Senate for questioning. The banks were in a crucible. Surely lessons had been learned?

And yet, the spikes kept showing up. If the fund manager was right, while senior executives were begging for forgiveness and rates traders were forlornly packing up their desks, the forex traders on the other side of the floor were carrying on as though nothing had happened. After some digging we found out that:

- The foreign-exchange market is the biggest in the world by some margin. It's a tidal wave of money. With more than $5 trillion changing hands each day, it would take some serious might to move it.
- More than 50 percent of the market was in the hands of just four banks including UBS, Citigroup and Barclays, the same institutions at the center of the Libor scandal. The top 10 firms controlled over 75 percent.[4] That's some serious might.

- Trading at the banks was undertaken by a relatively small number of people who knew each other socially and communicated throughout the day.
- Regulation of the foreign-exchange market was minimal, even after the crisis. In the words of one trader, it was like the Wild West.

Eventually we tracked down a disgruntled senior forex trader willing to talk.[5] After 20 years in the industry he felt jaded. Cheating at the fix was rife, he said. He'd seen it with his own eyes: Banks coming together on chat rooms and pushing rates around by sharing their positions and agreeing to buy and sell at exactly the same time—an illegal practice known as "banging the close".

Once that first domino fell, others began to topple more easily. In the end we found half a dozen individuals with firsthand experience of currency rigging. On June 12, 2013, we published an article with the headline: "Traders Said to Rig Currency Rates to Profit Off Clients".[6]

The story was picked up around the world. We were interviewed on television and radio. After refusing to engage with our inquiries for weeks, the Financial Conduct Authority now claimed it had been looking into the issue all along, which made our whistleblower laugh.[7] Then came the blowback. Banks refused to comment and froze us out of meetings. Traders complained about our coverage. The most strident defenders of the industry were in the press. *The Wall Street Journal* ran an op-ed from a foreign exchange veteran pooh-poohing the allegations as conspiracy theory.[8]

But was it really that surprising? Banks had huge currency positions that profited or lost depending on where different rates ended up, so traders had an incentive to cheat. The benchmark was run by a private company with no power or motivation to punish anyone. And, as with Libor, there was practically no oversight of the process. All the ingredients were there. As Steve Obie at the CFTC had put it: "Anytime there's human beings involved and there's the potential to make money, they do it."

Four months later, on Oct. 4, 2013,[9] someone shouted across the newsroom: "They've launched an investigation into FX!" The Swiss financial regulator had issued a statement saying it was looking into allegations of manipulation at multiple banks. Within a week, the U.S.

Justice Department had followed suit. By the end of the month, more than a dozen authorities from Europe, the U.S. and Asia had launched their own investigations. Then came the cull. Dozens of traders were pushed out and, unlike in Libor, many of them were senior figures within their institutions—business heads who sat on central bank committees and oversaw scores of people.

Details of precisely what the banks had been up to emerged gradually. If we'd made it up, Hollywood would have rejected it as too outlandish. Every day a band of senior currency traders at Barclays, Citigroup, Royal Bank of Scotland, UBS and JPMorgan came together on an invitation-only chat-room known as "The Cartel" and "One Dream One Team". There, they passed around confidential information on their clients' positions and discussed how they planned to "double-team" the market. Any members of the group with an opposing interest knew to offload their "ammo" ahead of the fix to an unsuspecting victim. Traders who weren't in the club were steamrollered mercilessly.

Cue another round of penalties, guilty pleas and hand wringing. Since our first story in June 2013, at least seven banks have been fined close to $10 billion for rigging currency rates.[10] Prosecutors have started bringing criminal charges against individuals. Similar investigations have uncovered evidence of tampering in benchmarks used in precious metals and oil.

Traders today complain of living in fear that chats from a bygone era will be dredged up and used against them. They paint a picture of a world where communications are monitored, compliance officers roam the trading floors and it's hard to make an honest living. Banks have finally got the picture, they claim. Market manipulation on the scale we've seen over the past few years is no longer possible.

Time will tell.

Notes

Introduction

1. BBA LIBOR: the world's most important number now tweets daily, British Bankers' Association, May 21, 2009, http://www.easier.com/25225-bba-libor-the-world-s-most-important-number-now-tweets-daily.html.
2. The lawyer initially refused to name his client, saying only that he was one of the traders identified in our article.

Chapter 1

1. In the 1988 movie *Rain Man*, Dustin Hoffman plays an autistic man who struggles to interact with people but is mathematically gifted, a talent put to work by his unscrupulous brother counting cards in Las Vegas casinos. Directed by Barry Levinson.

Chapter 2

1. Nick Hayes quoting Tania Zeigler, Twitter post, Sept. 1, 2015, 1:52 p.m., http://twitter.com/justice4tomh.
2. Regina v. Tom Hayes (2015), Hayes's testimony, Southwark Crown Court, London.

3. "Semiannual OTC derivatives statistics," Bank for International Settlements, 2015, http://stats.bis.org/statx/srs/table/d7?p=20092&c=.
4. Regina v. Tom Hayes (2015), Hayes's testimony, Southwark Crown Court, London.
5. In recent years UBS has been penalized by authorities around the world for facilitating money laundering, helping clients evade income tax, rigging the foreign exchange market and manipulating the price of precious metals. In 2011, rogue trader Kweku Adoboli racked up $2.3 billion in trading losses at the bank.
6. Tom Hayes, Serious Fraud Office interviews.

Chapter 3

1. New York-based Manufacturers Hanover was once one of the biggest U.S. lenders. It was acquired in 1992 by Chemical Bank, which subsequently became part of JPMorgan Chase.
2. Much of the biographical information in Chapter 3 comes from David Lascelles, *The Story of Minos Zombanakis*, Banking Without Borders (Athens: Economia, 2011), 24–100.
3. Ibid.
4. BIS Quarterly Review, December 2004.
5. The Bank of England raised its key interest rate 10 percentage points between November 1977 and November 1979. Bank of England, http://www.bankofengland.co.uk/boeapps/iadb/Repo.asp.
6. The CME's method for calculating the interbank rate was actually harder to game than Libor. It involved a random survey of banks, which were asked at what rate they were willing to lend to prime banks. No bank knew whether it was going to be included in the pool.
7. Carrick Mollenkamp, Jennifer Ablan and Matthew Goldstein, "How gaming Libor became business as usual", Reuters, Nov. 20, 2012, http://uk.reuters.com/article/us-libor-fixing-origins-idUSBRE8AJ0MH20121120 and CME data.
8. Ibid.
9. Andrew Verstein, a lecturer at Yale Law School, showed that one bank acting alone could move Libor. His calculations formed the basis of Liam Vaughan's and Katie Linsell's, "Libor Flaws Allowed Banks to Rig Rates Without Conspiracy", Bloomberg, July 16, 2012, http://www.bloomberg.com/news/articles/2012-07-16/libor-flaws-allowed-banks-to-rig-rates-without-conspiracy.
10. "Adjustable-Rate Mortgages and the Libor Surprise", Federal Reserve Bank of Cleveland, https://www.clevelandfed.org/newsroom-and-events/publications/economic-commentary/economic-commentary-archives/2009-economic-commentaries/ec-20090109-adjustable-rate-mortgages-and-the-libor-surprise.aspx.

Chapter 4

1. Regina v. Tom Hayes, Hayes's testimony.
2. A hedge is a trade designed to reduce or eliminate the risk of losses arising from a transaction. An investor in Apple, for example, may wish to protect himself from the possibility that the whole market tanks by shorting the S&P 500.

Chapter 5

1. Tom Hayes, SFO interviews.
2. David Enrich, "The Unraveling of Tom Hayes", *The Wall Street Journal*, Sept. 13, 2015, http://graphics.wsj.com/libor-unraveling-tom-hayes/1.
3. Regina v. Darrell Read, Colin Goodman, Danny Wilkinson, Terry Farr, James Gilmour and Noel Cryan (2015), Read's testimony, Southwark Crown Court.
4. "Order: ICAP Europe Limited", Sept. 25, 2013. http://www.cftc.gov/idc/groups/public/@lrenforcementactions/documents/legalpleading/enficaporder092513.pdf.
5. Regina v. Darrell Read, Colin Goodman, Danny Wilkinson, Terry Farr, James Gilmour and Noel Cryan (2015), Read's testimony, Southwark Crown Court.
6. Regina v. Tom Hayes, Hayes's evidence.
7. Regina v. Darrell Read, Colin Goodman, Danny Wilkinson, Terry Farr, James Gilmour and Noel Cryan (2015), Farr's testimony, Southwark Crown Court.
8. "Final Notice: David Caplin", Financial Conduct Authority, Jan. 22, 2015, https://www.fca.org.uk/static/documents/final-notices/david-caplin.pdf.
9. Ibid.
10. "Final Notice: Martin Brokers", Financial Conduct Authority, May 15, 2014, https://fca.org.uk/static/documents/final-notices/martin-brokers-uk-ltd.pdf
11. Regina v. Tom Hayes, evidence.
12. Regina v. Tom Hayes, testimony.
13. Tom Hayes, SFO interviews.
14. Regina v. Tom Hayes, Hayes's testimony.
15. Ibid.
16. Regina v. Darrell Read and Others, evidence.
17. Regina v. Tom Hayes, evidence.
18. Regina v. Darrell Read and Others, Goodman's testimony and witness statement.
19. Regina v. Darrell Read and Others, evidence.

Chapter 6

1. Mollenkamp wasn't the first journalist to highlight problems with Libor. On Sept. 25, 2007, Gillian Tett of the *Financial Times* published a piece titled "Libor's value is called into question", which reported suggestions the rate was "no longer offering such an accurate benchmark of borrowing costs". Tett

stopped short of suggesting banks were deliberately lying, http://www.ft.com/cms/s/0/8c7dd45e-6b9c-11dc-863b-0000779fd2ac.html.

2. "BIS Quarterly Review March 2008: International banking and financial market developments", BIS, http://www.bis.org/publ/qtrpdf/r_qt0803.pdf.
3. Scott Peng, Chintan Gandhi and Alexander Tyo, "Special Topic: Is LIBOR broken?", *Citigroup*, April 10, 2008, file: //corp.bloomberg.com/lo-dfs/users/lvaughan6/Downloads/citigroup%20is%20Libor%20broken.pdf.
4. Based on the recollection of former colleagues.
5. Carrick Mollenkamp and Mark Whitehouse, "Study Casts Doubt on Key Rate", *The Wall Street Journal*, May 29, 2008, http://www.wsj.com/articles/SB121200703762027135.
6. Mark Gilbert, "Barclays Takes a Money Market Beating", Bloomberg, Sept. 3, 2007, http://www.silverbearcafe.com/private/beating.html.

Chapter 7

1. BBA filings with Companies House.
2. Regina v. Tom Hayes, evidence.
3. Regina v. Tom Hayes, John Ewan's testimony.
4. Regina v. Tom Hayes, evidence.
5. The revelations may actually have cost borrowers money. On a 30-year £1 million mortgage tied to Libor, the two-day increase equated to an extra £146 a month.
6. "Meeting of the Federal Open Market Committee on April 29–30, 2008", Federal Reserve, http://www.federalreserve.gov/monetarypolicy/files/FOMC20080430meeting.pdf.
7. Peter Taylor, "Libor credibility questioned as credit crunch deepens", *Daily Telegraph*, April 17, 2008, http://www.telegraph.co.uk/finance/newsbysector/banksandfinance/2788384/Libor-credibility-questioned-as-credit-crunch-deepens.html.
8. Carrick Mollenkamp, "Libor surges after scrutiny does, too", *The Wall Street Journal*, April 18, 2008, http://www.wsj.com/articles/SB120846842484224287.
9. Regina v. Darrell Read and Others, evidence.
10. Peter Madigan, "Libor under attack", *Risk Magazine*, June 1, 2008, http://www.risk.net/risk-magazine/feature/1497684/libor-attack.
11. "Treasury—Minutes of Evidence", U.K. Treasury Select Committee, May 13, 2008, http://www.publications.parliament.uk/pa/cm200708/cmselect/cmtreasy/536/8051305.htm.
12. Regina v. Tom Hayes, evidence.
13. In July 2014, Lloyds Banking Group was fined after four of its traders manipulated the BBA Sterling Repo Rate to reduce the fees the bank had to pay

under the Special Liquidity Scheme. "Final Notice: Lloyds Bank plc and Bank of Scotland plc", Financial Conduct Authority, July 18, 2014, https://www.fca. org.uk/static/documents/final-notices/lloyds-bank-of-scotland.pdf.

14. "Fixing Libor: some preliminary findings (Written evidence)", U.K. Treasury Select Committee, Aug. 18, 2012, http://www.parliament.uk/documents/ commons-committees/treasury/Fixing-LIBOR-evidence2.pdf.

15. "Order: CFTC v. Barclays PLC et al", CFTC, June 27, 2012, http://www.cftc. gov/idc/groups/public/@lrenforcementactions/documents/legalpleading/ enfbarclaysorder062712.pdf.

16. "There's a tail of contracts that may take 10, 20, 50 years to run off which use Libor as an undefined term, because nobody felt it needed defining. The more changes you make, the more likely it is that somebody will be able to argue this is a material change to their contract," Simon Gleeson, a partner at law firm Clifford Chance in London, taken from Liam Vaughan and Gavin Finch, "Libor Guardians Said to Resist Changes to Broken Rate", Bloomberg, June 28, 2012, http://www.bloomberg.com/news/articles/2012-06-25/libor-guardians-said -to-resist-changes-to-broken-benchmark-rate.

17. "Fixing Libor: Some Preliminary Findings", U.K. Treasury Select Committee, Aug. 18, 2012, http://www.publications.parliament.uk/pa/cm201213/ cmselect/cmtreasy/481/48102.htm.

18. Several banks approached the BBA and asked to be removed from the Libor panels because of the possibility of reputational damage if they carried on quoting rates.

19. On the same day, ICAP launched a rival benchmark interest rate. Like Libor, the New York Funding Rate was based on a poll of the largest banks, but unlike Libor, banks' individual submissions were not published in order to eliminate any signalling effect arising from publicly posted levels. The NYFR was collected at 10 a.m. New York time, when trading in the dollar market was at its most liquid, compared with Libor, which was determined before U.S. markets opened. Ultimately, the NYFR failed. Despite the obvious flaws in Libor, the benchmark had become so ingrained in derivatives markets that participants continued to write it into contracts even as banks were receiving record fines. The ICAP rate was quietly scrapped in August 2012, when banks on the panel refused to continue providing estimates.

Chapter 8

1. Tom Hayes, SFO interviews.
2. Ibid.
3. At least two Libor submitting banks' submissions mirrored the brokers' suggestions 80 percent of the time in 2008. "Order: ICAP Europe Limited", Sept. 25, 2013 http://www.cftc.gov/idc/groups/public/@lrenforcementactions/ documents/legalpleading/enficaporder092513.pdf.

4. There is no suggestion Goldman Sachs was aware of Hayes's efforts to rig Libor when they tried to hire him. Goldman Sachs wasn't on any Libor-setting panels. The firm declined to comment.

5. Tom Hayes, SFO interviews.

6. Regina v. Tom Hayes, evidence.

7. Ibid.

8. Hayes said during his trial that he got approval from his boss Mike Pieri for the wash trade. Regina v. Tom Hayes, testimony.

9. Tom Hayes, SFO interviews and ibid.

10. Regina v. Tom Hayes, evidence.

11. Tom Hayes, SFO interviews.

12. Regina v. Tom Hayes, evidence.

13. Generally the traders would pay for their own flights. Everything else was paid for by the broker.

14. "Final Notice: David Caplin", FCA.

15. Regina v. Tom Hayes, evidence.

16. Kieran Corcoran, "'Wolf of Shenfield' broker who was shot last month hospitalized again on first day back at office after gang of prankster colleagues crept up behind him and shouted BANG", *Daily Mail*, Feb. 20, 2014, http://www.dailymail.co.uk/news/article-2563628/Wolf-Shenfield-shot-masked-man-train-station-hospital-pranksters-work-crept-shouted-BANG.html.

17. Regina v. Tom Hayes, evidence, testimony.

18. Regina v. Tom Hayes, evidence.

19. Regina v. Darrell Read and Others, evidence.

20. Regina v. Tom Hayes, evidence.

Chapter 9

1. Gensler is worth "as much as $61,745,000", based on public disclosures. Sophie Gilbert, "Who Are the Wealthiest Members of the Obama Administration?", *The Washingtonian*, March 27, 2009, http://www.washingtonian.com/blogs/capitalcomment/1600-pennsylvania-avenue/who-are-the-wealthiest-members-of-the-obama-administration.php.

2. Mara Der Hovanesian, Bloomberg, Nov. 17, 2002, http://www.bloomberg.com/bw/stories/2002-11-17/the-gensler-twins-identical-dont-you-believe-it.

3. Izabella Kaminska, "Libor is Useless", *Financial Times*, June 22, 2009, http://ftalphaville.ft.com//2009/06/22/58316/libor-is-useless/.

4. "FSA—Internal Audit Report: A review of the extent of awareness within the FSA of inappropriate LIBOR submissions—management response", March 2013, http://www.Fca.org.uk/your-fca/documents/fsa-ia-libor-management-response.

Chapter 10

1. "The Unraveling of Tom Hayes", *The Wall Street Journal*.
2. Regina v. Darrell Read and Others, evidence.
3. In an October 2008 e-mail to his boss complaining about Hayes's interference, Darin wrote: "One of the things that we signed up for when UBS agreed to join the fixing panel was the condition that fixing contributions shall be made regardless of trading positions." Regina v. Tom Hayes, evidence.
4. In 2008, the order was changed and the rate-setters were told to make their submissions "within the pack". Regina v. Tom Hayes, evidence.
5. Ibid.
6. Ibid.
7. David Enrich, "Rate-Rig Spotlight Falls on 'Rain-Man'", *The Wall Street Journal*, Feb. 8, 2013, http://www.wsj.com/articles/SB1000142412788732 4445904578285810706107442.
8. The communication would go on to serve as a central plank of the SFO's case against Hayes. Regina v. Tom Hayes, evidence.
9. No evidence was produced during the broker trial that Cryan passed on Hayes's requests to his cash desk. Regina v. Darrell Read and Others, evidence.
10. Regina v. Darrell Read and Others, evidence.
11. Regina v. Tom Hayes, testimony.
12. Hayes said Pieri knew that UBS had been approached earlier that year by the CFTC as part of the agency's investigation into dollar Libor. Regina v. Tom Hayes, testimony.
13. The decision to take Libor-setting out of the hands of the cash traders came after the BBA issued fresh guidance on how Libor should be set without reference to any bank's trading positions. Ibid.

Chapter 11

1. "Order: CFTC v. Barclays PLC et al", CFTC.
2. The call was described in detail by several people who heard it. The CFTC, the FCA and the Justice Department declined Freedom of Information requests for a copy of the recording or a transcript. Authorities in the U.S. considered including a reference to the conversation in their settlements with Barclays but concluded that it raised more questions than it answered.
3. Martin Taylor, "I too fell for the Diamond myth", *Financial Times*, July 8, 2012, https://next.ft.com/content/1385fc54-c699-11e1-963a-00144feabdc0.
4. "Regular OTC Derivatives Markets Statistics", BIS, Nov. 13, 2000, http://www.bis.org/publ/otc_hy0011.htm.
5. Centre for Economics and Business Research bonus data, http://www.cebr.com/.

6. "The FSA's report into the failure of RBS", U.K. House of Commons, Oct. 19, 2012, http://www.publications.parliament.uk/pa/cm201213/cmselect/cmtreasy/640/640.pdf.

7. Documents released by Barclays in July 2012 show the issue of Libor lowballing came up in conversations with the FSA, the Federal Reserve Bank of New York, the BBA and the Bank of England, https://www.home.barclays/content/dam/barclayspublic/docs/InvestorRelations/IRNewsPresentations/2012News/03-july-supplementary-information-on-libor.pdf.

8. Hank Paulson, "On the Brink: Inside the race to save the collapse of the global financial system", *Business Plus*, Feb 1, 2010.

9. Lehman administrator Alvarez & Marsal sued Barclays, claiming much of the profit came from Barclays secretly transferring valuable Lehman assets to its balance sheet that it had no claim to. The case settled in 2015.

10. Diamond's relationship with Mervyn King, by contrast, was strained, according to sources close to the two men. Diamond had apparently offended the governor by criticizing the Bank of England in the press for not intervening earlier to save the financial system.

11. E-mails released by Bank of England, July 6, 2012, following Freedom of Information request by John Mann MP, http://www.bankofengland.co.uk/publications/Documents/foi/disc170712a.pdf.

12. Lloyds was itself the product of a government-brokered shotgun wedding the previous month between British banks Lloyds TSB and Halifax Bank of Scotland.

13. Damian Reece, "Eric Daniels on HBOS: We did the country a great service...," *The Daily Telegraph*, Aug. 7, 2010, http://www.telegraph.co.uk/finance/financetopics/profiles/7932095/Eric-Daniels-on-HBOS-We-did-the-country-a-great-service....html.

14. Robert Peston, "All change at RBS", BBC website, Oct. 11, 2008, http://www.bbc.co.uk/blogs/thereporters/robertpeston/2008/10/all_change_at_rbs.html.

15. Barclays had in fact twice been forced to take out high-interest short-term loans from the Bank of England's emergency liquidity scheme in August 2007. In a statement at the time it said it was "flush with liquidity" and attributed the move to a technical problem. Ashley Seager, Larry Elliott and Julia Kollewe, "Barclays admits borrowing hundreds of millions at Bank's emergency rate", *The Guardian*, Aug. 30, 2007, http://www.theguardian.com/business/2007/aug/31/money.

16. "Email Between Mr Tucker and Jeremy Heywood", Bank of England, July 9, 2012, http://www.bankofengland.co.uk/publications/Documents/other/treasurycommittee/financialstability/emailsbetweenptjh.pdf.

17. It's interesting to note that the conversation took place as the BBA was finalizing its consultation paper on the Libor-setting process. The document, produced in collaboration with the Bank of England, refuted suggestions that banks

were lowballing Libor, claiming the allegations stemmed from a lack of under-standing among the press.

18. Letter from the Governor of the Bank of England to the Chairman of the Committee, dated Nov. 24, 2009, U.K. House of Commons, http://www.publications.parliament.uk/pa/cm200910/cmselect/cmtreasy/181/09121504.htm.

19. Both Tucker and King would claim during the Treasury Select Committee's Libor hearings two years later that they did not know that banks were low-balling their Libor submissions.

20. "Fixing Libor: Some Preliminary Findings".

21. "Evidence from Bob Diamond", Treasury Select Committee, http://www.parliament.uk/documents/commons-committees/treasury/Treasury-Committee-04-July-12-Bob-Diamond.pdf.

22. Andrea Jezovit, "Finance: Peak performer", *Canadian Business*, Oct. 13, 2008, http://www.canadianbusiness.com/business-strategy/finance-peak-performer/.

23. "Fixing Libor: Some Preliminary Findings".

24. "Barclays announces capital raising", Barclays, Oct. 31, 2008, http://www.newsroom.barclays.co.uk/r/1460/barclays_announces_capital_raising_-_correction_to_weblink.

25. Johnson pleaded guilty to conspiracy to defraud relating to the rigging of Libor and was sentenced to four years.

Chapter 12

1. As Breuer explained in a 2013 PBS documentary about the Justice Depart-ment's record on the crisis: "In a criminal case... I have to prove not only that you made a false statement but that you intended to commit a crime, and also that the other side of the transaction relied on what you were say-ing. And frankly, in many of the securitizations and the kinds of transactions we're talking about, in reality you had very sophisticated counterparties on both sides." Jason Breslow, "Lanny Breuer: Financial Fraud Has Not Gone Unpub-lished", Frontline, Jan. 22, 2013, http://www.pbs.org/wgbh/frontline/article/lanny-breuer-financial-fraud-has-not-gone-unpunished/

2. Justice officials interviewed for this book cited the cautionary example of accounting firm Arthur Anderson, which lost its license in 2002 after it was criminally charged with obstruction of justice relating to its role as auditor to Enron. The charges were later overturned, but by then the company was out of business, costing 85,000 people their jobs.

3. Both men have since returned to the firm.

4. The Stevens case provided a constant backdrop to the criminal division during the early years of the Libor investigation. Thousands lined the streets ahead of

Stevens' funeral in August 2010. A month later, Nick Marsh, one of the attorneys who led the investigation, committed suicide at 37. When the report into the case was eventually published in March 2012, it was damning. In particular it criticized the decision to strip responsibility for running the trial from the prosecutors who had built the case over several years and hand it to senior managers.

5. Marsh was on secondment from the CFTC at the time.
6. Tucker was interviewed voluntarily. The U.K. regulator's unwillingness to scrutinize either the Bank of England or the BBA was a constant source of frustration for its counterparts in Washington, according to investigators.
7. The Conservative Party formed a coalition government with the Liberal Democrats.

Chapter 13

1. Regina v. Tom Hayes, evidence.
2. Regina v. Darrell Read and Others, Laurence Porter's testimony.
3. Regina v. Tom Hayes, evidence.
4. Hayes claimed in court that he hadn't read the e-mail. Regina v. Tom Hayes, testimony.
5. Ibid.
6. Regina v. Tom Hayes, testimony of Porter.
7. "Axe" is banker parlance for a trading position, as in "an axe to grind".
8. Citi was also fined $2 billion by regulators for its involvement in rigging the foreign exchange market in 2014.
9. Hayes couldn't remember Thursfield's name when asked about the meeting by SFO investigators. He thought Thursfield was a bit standoffish but didn't get the impression that he disliked him. Hayes, SFO interviews.
10. Regina v. Tom Hayes, evidence.
11. Regina v. Darrell Read and Others, Read's testimony.
12. Regina v. Tom Hayes, evidence.
13. Hayes claimed he was shocked by Adolph's comment as the Deutsche Bank trader had never refused to help him before. Regina v. Tom Hayes, testimony and evidence.
14. Hayes claimed he spoke to Porter on the phone on the evening of March 3, 2010, and Porter agreed to lower Citigroup's Libor submission. Porter denied any such conversation took place and said the rate was lowered to reflect market conditions. Regina v. Tom Hayes, evidence and testimony of Porter and Hayes.
15. Hayes, SFO interviews.
16. Ibid.
17. Regina v. Tom Hayes, Porter's testimony.
18. Regina v. Tom Hayes, testimony.

19. Conversation based on Hayes's recollection of the meeting when on the stand. Ibid.
20. Ibid. Citigroup claimed the decision to allow Hayes to keep the bonus was made before the meeting due to Japanese employment law.

Chapter 14

1. Regina v. Tom Hayes, evidence.
2. The CFTC complained repeatedly about UBS's lack of cooperation with the investigation, according to sources at the agency.
3. E-mails reproduced during Hayes's trial. None of the managers involved in the discussion disciplined Hayes or escalated the matter to compliance. Kengeter left the bank in February 2013, days after *The Wall Street Journal* published an article quoting e-mails he'd sent to his executives instructing them to do their best to hold on to Hayes. Enrich, "Rate-Rig Spotlight Falls on 'Rain-Man'".
4. "Order: UBS AG", CFTC.
5. Allen & Overy also represented several other banks implicated in Hayes's conspiracy, so would have been conflicted if it continued to represent UBS.
6. Pete Brush, "Most admired attorneys: Gary Spratling". *Law 360* news service, Aug. 26, 2010, http://www.law360.com/articles/189690/most-admired-attys-gibson-dunn-s-gary-spratling.
7. UBS potentially escaped hundreds of millions of dollars in fines after securing leniency agreements from competition authorities around the world.
8. Deutsche Bank subsequently fired Adolph and withheld his bonuses from prior years. Adolph sued the bank. The case settled out of court.
9. Land registry records listed no mortgage when the house was first bought. The couple subsequently took out a mortgage and transferred ownership into Sarah Tighe Hayes's name.
10. Caroline McGhie, "Britain's Top 10 Richest Suburbs", *Daily Telegraph*, Dec. 21, 2007, http://www.telegraph.co.uk/finance/property/investment/3360057/Property-in-the-suburbs-Britains-top-10-richest-suburbs.html.
11. "The Unraveling of Tom Hayes", *The Wall Street Journal*.
12. Building application filings, land registry records and real estate particulars.
13. Regina v. Tom Hayes, character witness.

Chapter 15

1. "Statement of Facts", Department of Justice, June 27, 2012, http://www.justice.gov/iso/opa/resources/9312012710173426365941.pdf.
2. Deutsche Bank, by contrast, did not settle with regulators until April 2015, and was accused of dragging its feet and misleading investigators. It was hit with fines totaling $2.5 billion, which included levies for time-wasting and

evasion. Suzi Ring, "Deutsche Bank Misstatements and Dawdling Almost Double U.K. Fine", Bloomberg, April 23, 2015, http://www.bloomberg .com/news/articles/2015-04-23/deutsche-bank-misstatements-and-dawdling -almost-double-u-k -fine.

3. Corporations historically feared guilty pleas because they had serious consequences, such as losing one's license, or being excluded from lucrative government contracts. Those concerns have dissipated in recent years, with many firms that pleaded guilty getting waivers that have allowed them to avoid major disruptions to their businesses.

4. Mackey's became a tradition. Every time the CFTC settled with a bank or broker over Libor, staff congregated at the pub.

5. One of the biggest frustrations of the Libor investigation was proving who lost out and by how much. Gensler assigned an economist named Andrei Kirilenko to the task but after several months the former Massachusetts Institute of Technology professor concluded it was impossible—there were too many unknown variables. Who could say for sure whether traders were doing each other's bidding, or just paying lip service? And how could you determine with any confidence what the correct rates should have been when there was no underlying market?

6. In fairness, the negotiations dragged on for months. When Barclays agreed to settle with the authorities in 2011, it had no way of knowing how febrile the atmosphere would become.

7. When Barclays's internal public relations people were told about Libor a few weeks before the settlement, they were shocked. Unlike the lawyers, they realized instantly how badly it would play out in the media.

8. The payout included at least £20 million tied to the sale of Barclays's investment-management arm BGI, which Diamond had previously run. The £63 million figure was disputed by Barclays at the time.

9. "Competition and Choice in the Banking Sector", U.K. Treasury Select Committee, Jan. 11, 2011, http://www.publications.parliament.uk/pa/ cm201011/cmselect/cmtreasy/uc612-vi/uc61201.htm.

10. Letter from FSA chairman Adair Turner to Agius, April 2012, "Fixing Libor: Some Preliminary Findings", Treasury Select Committee.

11. Harry Wilson and Richard Tyler, "Bank mis-selling victims: from the chippy to the small hotel", *Daily Telegraph*, March 10, 2012, http://www.telegraph.co.uk/ finance/newsbysector/banksandfinance/9135986/Bank-mis-selling-victims- from-the-chippy-to-the-small-hotel.html.

12. Bruno Iksil's office was half a mile from the Barclays headquarters in Canary Wharf. His trading cost JPMorgan $6.2 billion.

13. Brooke Masters and Kara Scannell, "Barclays boss discussed Libor with BOE", *Financial Times*, July 1, 2012, http://www.ft.com/cms/s/0/94a88010- c37c-11e1-966e-00144feabdc0.html#axzz3t4dIRSpw.

14. Diamond and Del Missier were both questioned about the conversation by the Treasury Select Committee.
15. Sants went on to join Barclays as head of compliance and regulatory relations in January 2013. Less than a year later he left, citing "exhaustion and stress".
16. Bailey said he had "read the Riot Act" to Barclays. "Fixing Libor: Some Preliminary Findings", Treasury Select Committee.
17. Both men were rejected in favor of Mark Carney, the governor of the Bank of Canada.
18. Unlike Diamond, who relinquished all his deferred bonuses and deferred consideration, Del Missier negotiated an £8.75 million severance package.
19. "Fixing Libor: Some Preliminary Findings", Treasury Select Committee, Aug. 18, 2012.
20. Tucker left the Bank of England after more than 30 years in autumn 2013. He is currently a senior fellow at Harvard Kennedy School of Government.
21. Brooke Masters, George Parker and Kate Burgess, "Diamond Let Loose Over Libor", *Financial Times*, July 4, 2012.

Chapter 16

1. Regina v. Tom Hayes, testimony and evidence.
2. Regina v. Darrell Read and Others, evidence.
3. *The Wheatley Review*, written by the newly appointed head of the FSA, Martin Wheatley, was published in September 2012. It concluded that Libor was "severely damaged" and would need to be overhauled to restore confidence in the benchmark. Proposed reforms included using trading data to verify submissions, stripping responsibility for oversight of the rate from the BBA and subjecting the process to statutory regulation. It stopped short of recommending terminating Libor altogether, https://www.gov.uk/government/uploads/system/uploads/attachment_data/file/191762/wheatley_review_libor_finalreport_280912.pdf.
4. "The Unraveling of Tom Hayes", *The Wall Street Journal*.
5. Ibid.
6. Regina v. Tom Hayes, testimony.
7. Correspondence between the U.S. and U.K. authorities, and Hayes's lawyers. Regina v. Tom Hayes, evidence.
8. Regina v. Tom Hayes, testimony.
9. Enrich, "Rate-Rig Spotlight Falls on 'Rain Man'".
10. Regina v. Tom Hayes, testimony.
11. "The Unraveling of Tom Hayes", *The Wall Street Journal*.
12. Regina v. Tom Hayes, evidence.
13. Regina v. Tom Hayes, testimony.
14. "The Unraveling of Tom Hayes", *The Wall Street Journal*.

15. Hayes talked about meeting Sherrard during his trial, when he was asked about his decision to fight the charges against him. Sherrard declined to comment on their interactions.
16. Hayes's lawyers said during his appeal that the decision to transfer the house to Sarah's name was to release funds to pay for the legal bills.
17. Regina v. Tom Hayes, testimony.

Chapter 17

1. "The Unraveling of Tom Hayes", *The Wall Street Journal*.
2. Ibid.
3. Chawla was assisted by Max Baines and Gillian Jones of Red Lion Chambers.
4. Hayes had switched both his solicitor and his barrister since his arrest in December 2012. One cast-off described him as a nightmare client, who always believed he knew the best course of action.
5. Kengeter denies any knowledge of wrongdoing.
6. The firm would go on to be sanctioned for offenses including money laundering, tax evasion, mortgage-backed securities fraud and manipulating currency markets.
7. Privately, a senior Justice Department official said one of his biggest regrets was not indicting the trade body.

Epilogue

1. WM/Reuters is a joint venture between State Street and Thomson Reuters.
2. The methodology has since been overhauled, including widening the window to five minutes.
3. Investors who manage "tracker funds" have to transact at the 4 p.m. WM/Reuters rates for technical reasons relating to the need to match indexes that are calculated using the benchmark. There's currently more than $3 trillion in such funds globally, according to Morningstar.
4. Euromoney Institutional Investor data, 2015.
5. Thanks to our talented colleague Ambereen Choudhury.
6. Liam Vaughan, Gavin Finch and Ambereen Choudhury, "Traders Said to Rig Currency Rates to Profit Off Clients", Bloomberg, June 12, 2013.
7. The FCA replaced the FSA as the U.K.'s financial regulator in April 2013.
8. Vincent Cignarella, "FX Math: Volume, Not Collusion, Likely Cause of 'Fix' Mayhem", *The Wall Street Journal*, Aug. 30, 2013, http://blogs.wsj .com/moneybeat/2013/08/30/fx-math-volume-not-collusion-likely-cause-of-fix-mayhem.
9. We followed the story a couple of months later with "Currency Spikes at 4 p.m. in London Provide Rate-Rigging Clues", which examined how frequently major spikes occurred in different currency pairs in the lead-up to 4 p.m. Liam

Vaughan and Gavin Finch, Bloomberg, Aug. 28, 2013, http://www.bloomberg.
com/news/articles/2013-08-27/currency-spikes-at-4-p-m-in-london-
provide-rigging-clues.

10. Matt Levine, "Bank FX Fine Scorecard (Follow Along at Home)",
Bloomberg, May 20, 2015, https://www.bloomberg.com/view/articles/2015-
05-20/bank-fine-scorecard-follow-along-at-home-.

Acknowledgments

This book is the result of more than 300 interviews carried out over 18 months: with traders and brokers as well as their friends and family members; with regulators, central bankers and investigators; with academics and journalists; and with lawyers, bank executives and public relations professionals. Occasionally we quote people directly, but for the most part, because of the sensitivity of the subject matter and ongoing legal proceedings, the conversations were conducted on the basis that we wouldn't reveal the identity of those we spoke to. We would like to thank each and every individual who gave up his or her time to help us.

We were also blessed with a mountain of documentary material to draw from, including evidence produced during the trials of Tom Hayes, the interdealer brokers and the Barclays traders. The trials provided a seemingly endless supply of e-mails, instant messages, text messages, testimony and recorded phone calls to pick over, which enabled us to recreate many events using the language of the actors involved. For other parts of the book, particularly sections relating to the Libor investigation and Barclays, contemporaneous records were not always available. In those instances we sought to describe events and conversations using the accounts of the individuals in the room, which were then put to all participants. Not all of the individuals elected to comment.

First and foremost, we wish to thank our editor at Bloomberg, Robert Friedman, who has walked every step of this journey with us. It is no exaggeration to say that without Robert's deft touch, unerring patience and wisdom, this project would never have made it off the ground. *Bloomberg Businessweek* editor Nick Summers joined the party late but had a big impact on the finished manuscript for which we are extremely grateful.

The book would not have been possible without the support of Bloomberg, which generously granted us leave and never balked when deadlines came and went. In particular, we'd like to thank Edward Evans, our esteemed skipper, as well as Otis Bilodeau, Christine Harper, Reto Gregori, Stryker McGuire, Matt Winkler, John Micklethwait and the indomitable Dan Hertzberg, whose enthusiasm for the chase still outshines any cub reporter's. Special thanks to Randy Shapiro for her faith in the project as well as her legal expertise, and to Adam Wolanski and Roger Field who helped us navigate legal waters while writing the book we wanted to write. And, of course, to Nathan Smith, the Brigand.

At Wiley, we wish to thank our editor Thomas Hyrkiel and the rest of the team for their hard work and persistence.

Some individual thank-yous, starting with Liam:

Writing this book was at times all-encompassing, and I'd like to thank my friends and family for bearing with me when I was only ever half there. Mum, Dad, Becca, Ollie, Addy and the rest of the clan—you're the best brood anyone could possibly ask for. Suzi—you have been a perfect blend of love, support, advice and distraction. Every author should have one. I love you dearly.

And Gavin:

I'd like to thank my fantastic wife, Cece, for her quiet patience and understanding throughout the writing of this book. Your wise counsel has, as ever, been invaluable. I also thank my children, Oscar and Milo, for being such a joy and source of happiness after many a long day writing. And a special thank you to Suzi for keeping Liam largely sane.

Liam Vaughan and Gavin Finch
August 2016

About the Authors

Liam Vaughan and **Gavin Finch** write about financial crime for Bloomberg and *Businessweek* in London. In 2013, they uncovered a global conspiracy to manipulate the $5 trillion a day foreign-exchange market, sparking investigations on three continents that to date have resulted in $10 billion in fines for banks including JPMorgan, Citigroup, Barclays and UBS. They won a Gerald Loeb Award in 2014 and the Harold Wincott Award for Financial Journalism in 2013.

Vaughan now lives with his fiancée Suzi and can be found on weekends cheering Arsenal football club. Finch lives with his wife, Cece, and two boys, Oscar and Milo, in Brighton.

Index